Sudras and the State Politics

Sudras and the State Politics

Dr Raj Kumar

KALPAZ

ISBN: 978-93-5128-246-4

Price: ₹ 850

First Published, 2017

Published by

Kalpaz Publications
C-30, Satyawati Nagar,
Delhi – 110052
E-mail: kalpaz@hotmail.com
Ph.: 9212142040

Printed at: G. Print Process, Delhi

Cataloging in Publication Data—DK
Courtesy: D.K. Agencies (P) Ltd. <docinfo@dkagencies.com>

Kumar, Raj *(College teacher of history)*, **author.**
Sudras and state politics / Dr Raj Kumar.
pages cm
Includes bibliographical references.
ISBN 9789351282464

1. Dalits—India—History. 2. Shudras—India—History. 3. Dalits—Political activity—India. 4. Shudras—India—Politics and government. 5. India—Politics and government. 6. World politics. 7. Comparative government. I. Title.

DS422.C3K86 2017 DDC 305.56880954 23

Contents

PART - II

Comparative Politics = Dalit History

Acknowledgement

I wish to express my gratitude to my Mamaji (Sh. Dharshan Lala and Sh Mangat Ram) of Jalandhar.

I am thankful to my wife Dr Shabnam Grewal (soul) as inspiration, who provided me enough wit to write down this book.

I owe thanks to Director, Amit Garg my publisher whose co-operation went on long way in publication of this document in time.

Foreword

The work done by Dr Raj Kumar on the topic of "*Sudras and the State Politics*" is a wonderful philosophy on "*Sabdawali*". For a long time, after independence 1947, *Politics* has been regarded as a study of the State = India or Bharat and its study involve with the activities of the democratic institution like U.S.A. and other state of the world as advance countries. Now this state (India is a progressive state in *Polities* and its identity has been originated from the three (3) Greek words of Aristotle (384 BC – 322 BC), that is *Polis* (city-state), *Polity* (govt.) and *Politics* (constitution). So, in the original Greek sense of 'Alexander the Great' and "Herodotus", the father of "History", they studied the social problems of the world and launched the historical phenomena in art of writings the "Dalit History"; to control the huge population of a country of state with the concept of "Sudra State of Mind" Prof Raj Kumar has not only made this work accessible to huge audiance; but has provided valuable information by correcting the "History and State Politics" by making the background and consulting the books of Dr Perminder Kour, head deptt. Of Political Science, GCW. Gandhi Nagar (Jammu), work entitled, "Western Political Thought and Comparative Politics"; as a new horizontal of knowledge; with thanks.

Dr Shabnam Grewal

Preface

It gives me immense pleasure for presenting this book entitled '*Sudra and the State Politics*' as a new discovery of the art historian, found in art of writing the Dalit-history as a Sufi-Saint scholar, where stands the ideology of Mebooba Mufti or Narendra Modi = Prostitution Mehkama.

"*Politics*" of the upper class society is based on 'rites and ritual' with muscle power and money power = black marketing idea. Who Were the *Sudras*? Challenge before them as scientific discovery of the "*Chamar Civilisation*" = Dand-niti through art of writing the Dalit-history. As Sharan Kumar Limbale, a Marathi writer writes that "*History, Controversies and Consideration*"; where stands the politics of the BJP = Gau Mata and the PDP = Burhan Wani Ke Kisay = Ego problem or ID problem called in formal education.

Dated:- 08-08-2016
Place:- Barnai

Dr Raj Kumar
H.O.D. History
GCW Gandhi Nagar, Jammu

Introduction

Rise of New Religions equivalent like that of '*Radha Soami*' and '*Nirangkari*', after 1947, they brought a great change in the lifestyles of the "*Sudras*". With the rising power of Muslims and Hindus communities, on the basis of population, they are in numbers than that of Dalits or Sudras. It is a new discovery of the art historian to find out the *truth* in art of writings the Dalit-history which has been distorted by the Brahmins of India and Pakistan from the beginning of the history = Vedic Age.

Now, we take the example of Aryans, "who were highly civilised people" as per the statement of R.S. Chaurasia (*History of Ancient India*; pp. 12-14). The general opinion of the public at present they were *Chamars* and used to live in Central Asia as well as Uttar Pradesh, Punjab, Sindh, Baluchistan, Maharashtra, Delhi and were known *Jative, Harwar, Valmikis, Pathans;* etc. In North India, they have been known as Aryans.

In the early Vedic period they were settled in Punjab, Sindh, Multan, Jammu and Kashmir as per again recorded by R.S. Chaurasia *(Ibid.)*. In later Vedic age, they widely spread to the Gangetic Valley = Uttar Pradesh State of mine = Dalit Samaj Ke Khoj + Athenian Democracy Ke Soch = Work is Worship theory; and love with the Living Deity = Medieval history. In local form, they are called *Churas* of "*Barnai*". The actual date of their coming is uncertain, why because, they were deprived from the formal education = Gurukul Theory during the Brahminical age. As soon as, they developed their mind and search out the food problem = Village Culture + City-State Ka differences and studied the literature of Dr B.R. Ambedkar = Dalit movement found not in Uttar Pradesh, but in other parts of State and abroad. The photograph of Dr B.R. Ambedkar was displayed with Barrack Obama in comparative analysis = Hillery Clinton. But his book '*Annihilation of Caste*', inspired the Dalit historian to write on state politics which initiated by him after the partition of India. He worked hard for the Dalit Community and preserved their rights through the Constitution of India + OBC Quota = no begging statement. Brahmins of India, they became beggers, why because, they have materialistic view in their life style and could not draft the "*Real*" history of India like that of Kalidas Ke Darame.

Social structure, of the Sudra society, it was in hell at that time, why because of sanctioned imposed by the Brahmins, that, they could not enter into the village of Brahmin, they were deprived from the social-status, and used to rearers animals like that of "*Chandra Gupta Maurya*" (322-298 B.C.). Chanakya took him at home and provided the education of "Kingship Theory" like that of Balban.

In the meanwhile, Alexander's invasions were took place as a Greek ruler from the Gilgit (Astore was his Kingdom). Political condition of "*Nandas*" were shattered, they were converted from Sudra to Kshatriyas as at present we see that political unity of BJP and PDP have been scattered, why because of the intution of the Jagmug Theory, author has started the campaign against the anti-Dalits to kill the Farooq Abdullah as a great sinner of the present senerio. Author has the "*Chalk and Boarding Method*". They have only adopted Iranian practice in their lifestyle as Satan or Hamim of the period = political monger.

The Greeks historians like Starbo, Arrain and Justin tell us that Indian coins were not round, but they were oblong bits of metal cut out of a strip and were "*punch marked*" = Race of Pandavas, according to A.C. Clayton (pp. 10-12), "*The Rig-Veda and Vedic Religion*".

Alexander marched upto the Beas, after his fight with Porus, Alexander marched eastward and a crossed the river Chenab Valley and reached the bank of Beas and fought a risky battle with Nandas (R.S. Chaurasia; p. 91).

In 323 B.C., Alexander crossed the Baluchistan, Persia and reached Babylonia, (Baghdad), where he was fell ill seriously and could not conquered the whole India, because of his early death. He was died at the age of hardly 33 years.

Moreover, many scholars who came to India from Greek such as Megasthense, Nearchos and Arrian, etc. have left valuable accounts of historical importance (R.S. Chaurasia; p. 93) in Indian history for the constructing of past = in present period.

Study shows that *Sudras* and *Brahmin* they used to work together during the time of Maurya, why, because that was the era of Buddhism. There is no caste-system. In the study, again, we learn that history distorted from the Mauryan period too.

Kautilya or Vishnu Gupta was the Prime Minister and great supporter of Chandra Gupta Maurya (322-298 B.C.) with the rising of Mauryan dynasty Greek Civilisation came into the contract of Chandra Gupta Maurya as a *Virsala* King = Dalit emperor.

***Rise of Magadha*:-** The early dynasty of Magadha that is Nanda, went into shrouded in darkness, due to the death of Alexander. Whereas, Mauryan King Ashoka founded Kashmir as a Buddhist State. As a V.A. Smith his rightly remarked and quoted the view of Mathew Arnold:-

"The East bowed low before the bast
In patient, deep disdain;
She let the legions thunder past, = Dr Shabnam Grewal.
And plunged in thought again." as a Buddhist view.

Dr R. K. Mookerji is of the view that Alexander invasion promoted the political unification of the country as Hitler made the unification of Germany. Small states which handicapped in unity were now merged in large ones and these conditions were favourable = shortly founded by Chandra Gupta Maurya (V.D. Mahajan; *Ancient India*; p. 105).

Ashoka (273-236 B.C.) was a great king not only in the history of India; but also of the whole world. "*Politic*" of the Sudra clan = Rai dynasty of Kashmir or Sindh has been based on Chamar thought as a political concept or as an objective of the life in human form to control the whole empire of India.

Dalit-King Ashoka killed 99 brothers and became the ruler of Kashmir=Burhan Wani + army personnels + 66 Youths, etc.

Politics was not originated by Chanakya, but was started by the wise king Ashoka to control the whole state of India as *Chamar-Thought* = Sudra State of mind. Author did work with sensible manner by publishing various books on the Nam-Theory after 2005, nobody was bother to listen the music of the Nam. "*History Repeat Itself*", it was the slogan of Chandra Gupta Maurya why Alexander left the valley of Gilgit and died in Babylonia = He was a fellow-friend of the unnatural history. Moreover, Greek-invasion under Alexander had remained limited, but this time Greeks succeeded in North India as far as the Ganga-Yamuna-Doab regions. However, there is no record for *Sakas* and *Demetrius* about their help. According to Herr Niese, "later development of Buddhism effected with the ideology of King Ashoka in Kashmir and Chandra Gupta Maurya recognised the suzerainty of Seleucus Nikator" as Nam. Where stands the ideology of NC, PDP, Congress and BJP as negative ruler = prostitute Mehkama. (V. D. Mahajan; p. 105).

Ashoka and the Buddhism was the new zeal of *Dharma*, that duties were defined by him to spread the Buddhism in abroad, as did by Nirankari Baba as well as by Baba Gurinder Singh Ji and his forefathers. Ashoka's place in history like that of Akbar and Samudra Gupta.

"*Politics*" is a Greek word originated from term *politicos* means of an action and wise in the circumstances as both Dr Raj Kumar and Dr Farooq Abdullah are different in their opinion, that they never thought about the 'reign of terror' in Kashmir. It will be expose through a novel named "*Kashmir Tragedy after the death of Burhan Wani*". a Drama Novel or drama has been wrote on this event to chase the power of the throne of Kashmir = Buddhasattva Ke Story.

Greek's history was different than that of Roman history. "Roman" means on the event of Burhan Wani, most of the Muslims, they were weeping, but author visualised the ideology of the anti-Dalit historians + political parties = prostitution Ka Dor led by Farooq Abdullah and Sonia Gandhi.

In the last, author wants to clear the defects in historical writing the Dalit history. From the very beginning history of India has been distorted in the light of beginning of Nanda to Mauryan dynasty. *Sudra's* politics is to provide the food, cloth and shelter as a progressive idea in history + New Society of India = mixed view.

There is no need of politics 'in' the Sudra State of mind

Money and social change is there in India, author needs positivism= Deyanat-dari Ka rule = Raj-Rishi Ke Sabita.

No doubt, number of civilisation after the Greeks, they developed in European countries, with idea of Nam + Sarasvati Civilisation of Akhnoor and Indus Valley. Now, Raj-Rishi Ki Sabita, based on true value + comparative analysis of Taoism including Muhamad Ghori and Ghazanavi Ke invasions, over north India + Prithiviraj Raso Ka Kalam = Ney dor Ke Suruat + Comparative politic of India Machiaveli (1469 - 1527) Ka Dor = Mughal Badshah, Shahjehan Ka Jamana = "*History Repeat Itself*" + Quranic verses of Holy Quran + Dampati resayte Ke Khoj = Nazla Chak Village Ke duty = manpasand Sud Kana.

J. S. Mill (1806-1873) Ka Vichar of Modern State = women equality + liberty. There is no need of the Purdha system = open war + authoritarian Ka rule and the State Politics = governing body of the Dalit Kings and his associatest+Pandava Kumba with the grace of almighty, author feels a great sense of pride = cheap mentality, but great demand of this book. (Sudras and the State Politics).

PART - I

WESTERN POLITICAL THOUGHT = NEW DISCOVERY OF THE DALIT KING AS KHALJI IMPERIALISM

Chapter - 1

A History of Greek Political Thoughts: A Profile, Ancient and Medieval

A number of civilisations existed in the ancient era with their own importance. Ancient Greek, ancient Egypt, ancient Rome, ancient India, ancient Japan, Scandinavia in Viking Times, Sparta and Persia were the prominent among them. Ancient Egypt is known by the Pyramids. World's first sanitation system, world's first dockyard, world's first sine table, numeral system especially zero (0) = infinite knowledge, world's oldest dam etc. are the greatest contributions of the Indian civilisation, Likewise the Chinese civilisation is famous for the games and elected government officials through merit instead of wealth and hereditary system. But the ancient Greek is the most influential civilisation of the world. Fifty three thousand words in this world have the Greek origin. Greek civilisation has contributed a lot in the field of arts, music, science, mathematics, games etc. the musical notation system, epic poetry, science of philosophy, humanism democracy, development of mathematics, automatic door, mythology, science of anthropology, coined money, the Olympic games, thermometer, tumbler locks, central heating, Greek fire geometry, first mechanical clock etc = Administrative Measures.

Thus, the Greek civilisation is the most important civilisation because the Greeks have preserved their national heritage and passed on their writing to the next generations. Hence, the Europeans have borrowed from the available the Greek philosophy i.e. why the Europeans are widely influenced by the Greek political thoughts = original view has been found in their philosophy.

A. Contribution of the Greek Political Thought to the World

In the opinion of Earnest Barker, "Political thought begins with the Greek. Its origin is connected with the calm and clear rationalism of the Greek mind." The Greeks were the first to present the political philosophy, political ideas and concepts in a systematic form which were, later on, borrowed and developed by the Europeans. The following are the important contributions of the Greek political thought to the world:

1. **Nature of City-State**: J.P. Suda and Satish Kumar's view, Meerut College, Meerut. The concept of city-state is the most-important contribution of the Greek political thought to the world because the word 'Politics' is derived from the Greek word 'Polis'which means city-state. It further means that the whole Greek politics revolves around the city-state. The information about 158 city-states with full-fledged constitutions and governments is found in the writings of Aristotle especially in his important work The "*Politics*".

   City-state was the area of a state consisted of 5040 citizens with direct legislation. People had direct contact with their rulers. The city-state was a classless state in which there were equal opportunities for all with full social honour and respect for everyone. It was a complete social organisation in which the citizens continuously participated in the state affairs.

   Greek city-state was a community, a true commonwealth republic. The people used to share a common life and common purposes as we enjoy this kind of life in our educational institutions, our work places etc. They discussed their problems and found the solutions and led respectful life or *res publica*.

   Greek states: Greece had two the most powerful and eminent states- Athens and Sparta. The functioning of Athens and Sparta had a great impact on the writings of Plato and Aristotle = Ethical in Nature.

2. **Nature of State**: The Greek philosophy is based on the nature of state. The Greek political thinkers = Ashoka

Angurana/AS gave a good account of the origin "*Bakat Ke line drawing*" and the end of the state. Plato's Ideal State, Aristotle's classification of government i.e. Monarchy, Aristocracy, Polity, Tyranny, Oligarchy and Democracy etc. have reflected the nature of the state in a very systematic order. Moreover, statements like, State is prior to man, State is as a supreme association, etc. are also reflected the nature, importance and functions of the state.

3. **Nature of Man**: The Greek thinkers were the first to consider man as a social animal. In the words of Aristotle, "Man is a social animal by nature. He who is unable to live in society because he is sufficient for himself must be either a beast or God." Thus, they were the first to disclose the social nature of man. For them, an isolated person was very dangerous for the state. He could not think positive for the society.
4. **Collection of Political Treatises**: The Greek political thought is characterised by a number of political and independent treatises such as *The Republic, The Laws, The Statesman, The Politics* etc. These treatises = Dalit History of the Jammu and Kashmir State + Pt. Kalhan Ke Rajatarangini are concerned with the study of political problems. No other ancient civilisation had produced political treatises in a purely political form except the treatises as the mixture of mythology and religious literature with the political ideas e.g. "*The Mahabharata*", "*The Ramayana*" etc. = '*History Repeat Itself*'.
5. **Educational System = History of modern India**: The Greek political thought has given importance to the education. They emphasised on the practical system of education. It believed in state-controlled educational system. It aimed at promoting self-control, patriotism, modesty, strength and sociability. It had close relationship with politics as Plato's philosopher-kings were the product of educational system = a community of Dalit-persons sharing in a common life + Raj-Rishi Ke Sabita.

6. **Greek Views on Political Concepts**: Greece has given the following views on political concepts:
   (a) **Democracy**: The concept of democracy has Greek origin which is, later on, borrowed and developed by the Europeans.
   (b) **Justice**: Justice plays an important role in the ancient Greek political thought especially it can be found in the writings of Plato. Platonic justice is based on morality.
   (c) **Citizenship**: For them, citizenship means direct participation in the management and activities of the state as a judge, as a legislator. Secondly, the possession of property and ownership of slaves are the other qualifications of the person to acquire citizenship. The slaves, resident aliens, foreigners, mechanics, labourers, old people, women and children were not considered as citizens.
   (d) **Believe in Inequality = Brahmin Mat**: They believed in inequality. For them, inequality was natural and permitted the dominance of the Greeks over barbarians. They were against the equality which was not an ideal thing. It was something unnatural, impractical and undesirable.
   (e) **Faith in Laws = Modern Radha Soami Mission**: The Greek political thinkers had firm faith in the laws. Aristotle is of the opinion that the prescription of law is the highest principle to be followed in a state. The sovereignty of the law makes the state secular the importance of law in the modern state given by the political scientists is the contribution of the ancient Greek thinkers.
7. **Methodology = Common Creed**: Inductive and deductive methods were used by the Greek thinkers. They attached great importance to discussion method in the form of 'dialects'. They also emphasised on reason also. The concept of idealism and realism, comparative method also important feature of the ancient Greek political thought.
8. **Role of Religion**: Both the state and the people had strong faith in worshipping the gods. There was no struggle between

the state and the church. It had given an idea of secularism of its own nature.

9. **Ideas about Law = Nam - history:** The Greek had a great respect for laws. It was the duty of every citizen to obey the laws of the land whether the laws were good for them or not, e.g. Socrates obeyed the laws of the land and sacrificed his life.

B. Different Political Thoughts in Greece Before Plato

There were different political thoughts in Greece before Plato such as:

- Political Thoughts of the Sophists
- Political Thoughts of Socrates
- Political Thought of the Cynics
- Political Thought of the Cyrenaics

1. **Political Thought of the Sophists**: The word 'Sophists' has been derived from the Greek word 'Sophiyes' which means 'learned'. Thus, the Sophists were a group of teachers such as Gorgias, Lycrophon, Hippias, Protogorus, Prodieus etc. who came to Athens from other cities. They were treated as foreigners by the Athenians. They aimed at imparting knowledge to all those who wished to learn. They charged heavy fees for imparting instructions. So, only the rich could afford their knowledge. They taught different subjects like political philosophy, logic, morals, and politics. Their teachings were based on the rhetoric method.

   The Sophists believed in the selfishness of man and considered the state as an artificial creation. They systematised the existing knowledge which was lying scattered and gave it a definite shape. They brought politics closer to reality. They also drew a clear line of difference between law and morality = Government system.

2. **Political Thought of Socrates (469-399 B.C.)**: Socrates was the teacher of Plato. He contributed a lot in the development of Greek political philosophy. He was born in

469 B.C. He was the son of an Athenian sculptor. He devoted most of his time to philosophical discussions. He had keen interest in performing the civic duties so as a result, he fought in the wars of Thrace and Delium as soldiers. He became the member of the Council at the age of 65. As the member of the Committee, he refused to support the illegal activities i.e. a close relationship between politics and ethics. He remained as the President of the Assembly. At the age of 70, he was tried by the Athenian court on the charge of corrupting the society. He sentenced to death in 399 B.C.

Socrates Contribution = Political Theory and Indian Politics: Socrates wrote nothing and whatever his knowledge the world knows is made available by his disciples like Plato, Xenophon, Isocrates etc. through their writings.

(a) **Views about Knowledge = Dr Bhagwan Das Ka Vichar**: Socrates was fully conscious of the value of knowledge. For him, "Virtue is knowledge." To discover this knowledge, he adopted dialectical method. His style of developing philosophical ideas was unique. He oftenly used to visit the market places and encouraged the people to discuss with him on different concepts like friendship, love, courage, justice, virtue etc. During this conversation, he provided them the opportunity to express themselves. A number of meaning and concepts came forward. Socrates brought out the defects in them and modified them. This process of point and counterpoint went on the till a really satisfactory definition was produced.

(b) **Knowledge is Virtue = New Discovery of the Dalit Education:** Knowledge is virtue is the most significant teaching of Socrates. For him, the real knowledge must be a matter of realisation in life. It is a power that brings about the transformation of personality. Soul is the main source of knowledge. When a man gets knowledge, it means, it is the qualification or excellence of his soul which results in action marked by that excellence. The excellent state of the soul is the highest happiness which a wise man attains. Thus, the term 'virtue' indicates the excellent working of the soul of which the moral quality may be an aspect.

(c) **Dialectical Method = Third Force that is, Dalits:** Socrates is the founder of the dialectical method based on question-answers and discussion. "*Truth*" can be reached only through discussion in which there must take place a conflict between two opposite points of view. The procedure of dialectic is governed by strict logical rules. The answer to the question must be in the fewest, clearest possible words. Both answer and question must be precise on every point. Socrates had learnt it from Zeno.

(d) **His view on State = Natural History:** He considers the State as natural institution. State is prior to the individual and the community. It aims at general welfare. For him, politics is an art so only the intellectual persons may rule the state. He believes in the ideal state where intellect and reason are utilised in the statecraft. In other words, he is in the favour of rule of Philosopher-kings.

(e) **His views on Law = Practical Wisdom:** For him, laws should be based on the moral principles so that they may guide the citizens who may respect them. This, for him, law is above the ruler and the ruled.

(f) **His views on Human Nature = Insaniyat Ka Dor:** According to Socrates, human nature consists of both instincts selfishness and urge to welfare. Selfishness is very harmful and urge to welfare is useful for him. Thus, the latter nature is the primary human nature.

3. **Political Thought of the Cynics = Chamar History:** The preaching and sacrifice of Socrates gave birth to a new ideology in Greece called as Cynicism. Antisthenes was the founder of this political thought. In spite of Cynicism, another political thought also developed, known as Cyrenaicism. Aristeppus was the main pioneer of Cyranaics ideology. Aristeppus resided at Cynics on the sea coast of Africa. Thus, the title names as Cyrenaics.

The Cynics Political Thought: The Cynics tried their best to extend Socratic wisdom all over the world. They pleaded for world citizenship. He was a contemporary of Plato. He wrote **Concerning Law and Cyrus or Concerning Monarchy.**

Contribution to Political Thought:

(a) **Return to Nature = Life Comes Life:** Cynics gave the slogan: "Back to Nature". They supported living in the lap of Nature away from the artificiality of society and state. Later on, Rousseau supported this cynic slogan in education.

(b) **Idea of World State = New Discovery of the Art Historian:** According to cynics, we are citizens of a world state. This idea was developed by Diogenes, according to whom all of us are citizens of a universal world state.

(c) **Concept of Individualism = Nam-Theory:** Cynics gave the concept of individualism in political thought for the first time. They were the strong supporters of individualism. For them, man is perfect himself. Self knowledge leads to human liberation, society or state is not necessary for him.

(d) **Cosmopolitarism = New Social Order:** They supported cosmopolitarism and world citizenship which were against the political ideology of Plato and Aristotle. Cynics were against the theory of city-states.

(e) **Brotherhoodness = French Scholar Ke Story:** They believed in universal brotherhood. They preached the whole world as one family, one state and one should fulfill his duties accordingly. This ideology had great impact on political thought.

4. **Political Thought of Cyrenaics**:

(a) **Self-Knowledge**: Man should aspire after liberation from worldly bondage. Self-knowledge alone can lead to it. Man can attain liberation by following Socratic dictum 'know thyself.

(b) **Secret of Pleasure Lies in the Present**: For them, the aim of man is the attainment of pleasure. The man should live only in the present in order to achieve and enjoy the maximum pleasure. He should not think of past or future. It can create pain for him. Thus, the present is the ultimate truth so live in present for maximum pleasure.

(c) **Importance to Customs**: They gave importance to customs as customs are based on traditions. Human aspirations and circumstances depend upon customs.

(d) **Rejection to Artificiality**: They seriously rejected the artificiality. They considered state and its laws as artificial. Man should attain self-knowledge and seek perfection.

Chapter - 2

Plato (427 B.C.-347 B.C.)

Plato was born in 427 B.C. in a noble Athenian family and launced the concept of Athenen democracy; work is worship and had royal blood running through his veins. His period was an era of great historical importance. When he was two years old, the great Athenian General Pericles died and Athens faced a humiliating defeat in the Poloponnesian War. He was the eyewitness of Macedonian militarism sweeping, defeat of Athens in wars against Spartas, the establishment of tyrannical rule of reactionaries and execution of his master Socrates by the reactionaries. All these incidents compelled him to write and to establish the rule of philosopher-king. He received the education from his great master Socrates for eight years. After the death of Socrates, Plato went on his journey through Egypt, Cyrene, Italy, Cieley etc. He travelled in different countries in order to observe their way of life, social and political structures and institutions and exchanging his ideas with other scholars of the different countries = *Old Buddhism + New Radha Soami Mission.*

After ten years of his journey, he returned to Athens and established an institution named as Academy or Gymnasium. He worked there as a teacher, a mathematician of the Nine natural numbers = Aryabhat Ke Soch and a philosopher. He imparted education to hundreds of illustrious disciples for 40 years and created dozens of dialogues up to his death at the age of 82.

Works of Plato = Life Statement

The political philosophy of Plato is mainly contained in The Republic (386 B.C.), The Statesman (360 B.C.) and The Laws (347 B.C.).

The problems individual and state are also discussed in The Apology and Crito. The Meno, The Protagoras and Gorgias. *The Phaedrus, The Phaedo, The Philebus, the Critias* etc. are another his important works.

Socrates Influence on Plato

In the words of Sabine, "The outstanding fact of Plato's intellectual development was his association as a Youngman with Socrates, and from Socrates, he derived what was always the controlling thought of his political philosophy, the idea that virtue is knowledge."

According to Prof. Ernest Barker, "Though Plato borrowed basic ideas from Socrates but he unfolded these ideas on his own way and reached his own conclusions. However, he admits that the image of his teacher never faded from his mind and he actually represents the greatest legacy bequeathed by Socrates to mankind."

These two statements reflect the influence of Socrates on Plato. It is very difficult to differentiate between the ideas of Socrates and Plato. Plato speaks in his dialogues through Socrates. Plato has borrowed the following doctrines from Socrates:

1. **Virtue is knowledge = Nam**: For Socrates, knowledge is for virtue. It consists of a collection of information and character formation in the sense that, after getting the knowledge, a person applies it on him which makes him strong. Otherwise, without practising it, it becomes useless and meaningless. Knowledge gives birth to the virtue of courage, temperance and justice etc. It was on the basic of this idea of Socrates, Plato developed his concept of Philosopher-king in his "***The Republic*".**
2. **Theory of Reality = Kalidas Ke Drame**: Socrates is of the opinion that reality lies in the world of ideas. According to him, "Beauty could exist without a beautiful thing." e.g. rose has a short life, but whenever we think of rose- number of qualities related to it- like its colour, fragrance, its utilisation as rose water etc. come in our mind and we enjoy. It means

that reality does not exist in philosophy presence but exists in ideas. And that world of ideas is the reality for him. Later on, Plato thought of an 'Ideal State' = Jammu and Kashmir State.

3. **Theory of Knowledge = True Vegetarian**: According to Socrates, there are two types of knowledge:
   (a) *Casual knowledge*
   (b) *True or real knowledge*
   (a) Casual knowledge means a belief or opinion of a person which can be changeable or shakable. It consists with fear also. It is temporary in nature.
   (b) True or real knowledge is permanent = Ravidas Ke Philosophy, scientific and based on reason. It is self-knowledge which one observes and implement on himself. It helps in character formation and personality development. It is permanent in nature. All the virtues depend upon knowledge.

   Plato also borrowed this theory of knowledge and applied it in his ideal state.
4. Dialectical Methods! Socrates invented the question answer method of philosophical discussion. Plato adopted this method in his dialogues. In this method, the inquirer explains the thoughts of various thinkers upon a problem and arrives at the truth by their constructive criticism.

Plato's Concept of Justice = New Social Order or Fatwa

Plato was the citizen of Athens. He was not satisfied the prevailing condition of Athens because of Athenian democracy and defected educational system. The educational system was under the control of Sophists who charged heavy fees for imparting instruction so only the rich could afford their knowledge. The main aim of ***The Republic*** is the discovering of the nature and types of justice. ***The Republic*** is also known as a treatise on justice. Another name for The Republic is Concerning Justice. In order to understand his justice, one should know the prevalent theories of justice.

Prevalent Theories of Justice

- Traditional Theory of Justice = Nam
- Radical Theory of Justice = Chamar Thought
- Pragmatic Theory of Justice = Sudra
- Rationalism = Reality Base Knowledge

1. **Traditional Theory of Justice**: The traditional theory of justice was given by Cephalus and Polymarchus. They were of the opinions:

   (a) Justice resides in speaking the truth in words and action

   (b) Pay one's debt

   In other words, it means justice is an art which gives good to friends and evil to enemies. It is based on tit for tat, principle.

   This theory is rejected by Plato following grounds:

   (a) If justice is an art, it should treat all members equally as a doctor does not differentiate between rich and poor; man and woman individual and criminal. All are patients for him.

   (b) It is very difficult to differentiate between friend and enemy. One's supposed friend can be a friend in appearance but in actual practice, he may be enemy to him.

   (c) To have a feeling of hatred or negative attitude towards enemy cannot be called justice. It is against the concept of justice.

2. **Radical Theory of Justice**: This theory of justice is supported by sophists like Thracymachas. According to Thracymachas:

   (a) Justice is the interest of the stronger.

   (b) It is directly related with the supreme authority (ruler) in the state. It means that justice prevails in the state according to the will of a ruler.

This theory of justice is again criticised by Plato on the following ground:

(a) To govern the state is an art. The ruler should run the state for the welfare of general masses.

(b) This theory of justice leads the ruler towards dictatorship where the justice lies to satisfy the ruler. And if man satisfies himself is against the wishes of the ruler because ruler is the strongest person in the state and according to this theory, justice is the interest of the stronger.

3. **Pragmatic Theory of Justice**: This theory of justice is given by Glaucon. For him, justice is the child of fear and interest of the weaker sections of the society = Dalit Samaj.

According to pragmatic theory of justice is not natural but an artificial, that is, called modern sciences, Physics, Chemistry, etc. People were weak in ancient period and were unable to oppose the strong = *Brahminical element*. Thus, they lived together as a sort of social contract and always prepared themselves neither to do injustice nor tolerate injustice = '*Gulistan Ke Story*'. (This theory reflects a theory of social justice which was later on developed as the Social Contract Theory.)

Plato again criticised this theory of justice on the following ways:

(a) Justice is not conventional or external. It is internal.

(b) It is not artificial but natural.

(c) It is not the interest of the weaker because there is no historical evidence in the evolution of human civilisation which gives us an idea of social contract.

4. **Rationalism = Religious Belief**: According to Socrates, justice is an art which aims at removing the evil from the state and building a healthy state. For example, an ideal teacher removes all the doubts and defects of the students and develops the capacity of their minds through his lectures and discussions. In the same way, a ruler is successful if he imparts justice to his subject and removes the

defects from them. In other words, justice is an art like artist who paints a picture for the sake of art without achieving selfish end and always trys to bring further improvement in his art.

Plato's Theory of Justice = Nam-History

Plato's justice is based on the rejection of the prevalent theories of justice. He has elaborated his theory of justice in his important work "***The Republic***". R.C. Majumdar ke Kitab: Ancient India. He has discussed the theory and nature of justice, its characteristics, political and social justice etc. in his book:

> Quality of soul = Big Bang Idea + New Discovery of the Ar and Rambi; and social justice = equality base knowledge of the Dalit race: He has discussed the nature of social justice in the form of a dialogue between Socrates and his friends in "***The Republic***". They discussed about the aim of human life, the structure of human personality and relationship between the individual and the society. Different persons have different capacities so one should develop one's own capacity. The human soul is consisted of three tendencies-knowledge, physical tendency and spiritual tendency. Spirit should rule over other tendencies. Thus, the spiritual person should rule in the state. Reason, courage, temperance and justice are the four ideal values.

Division of Society = Manusmriti Ke Dastana = Sungha Dynasty: On the basis on these ideal values, he has developed the concept of division of society into three classes:

	Classes	*Ideal values*
1.	Philosopher Kings	Reason
2.	Soldiers	Courage
3.	Peasants	Temperance

The important function of the state is to provide justice and maintain balance or harmony among reason courage and temperance. Thus, for Plato, Justice is the quality of soul.

Characteristics of Plato's Justice

The following are the important characteristics of Plato's justice:

1. **Inner Voice:** According to Plato, justice is innate. It is the quality of soul. It is an inner voice.
2. **Functional Specialisation:** Plato has divided the society on three classes—philosopher-kings, soldiers and peasantry class-on the basis of human tendencies. For him, justice consists in the fulfilling of duties by all these classes of the human history like Megh, Batwal, Barabales like Gulab Singh-Nirangkar Mission = Mahasha Baradari.
   (a) Philosopher-king—to exchange knowledge and rule over the state.
   (b) Soldiers—to protect the state.
   (c) General people—to do economic activities for the state.

   Thus, his justice is based on functional specialisation which reflects a state constitutes political power, muscular power and economic power.
3. **Social and Economic Justice = Reservation Quota:** On the basis of functional specialisation, he has classified justice into two important types of justice: social justice and economic justice.
4. **Individual Justice = Dr B.R. Ambedkar Ka Kiyal:** He has also thought for the individual or personal justice while giving his communism. He has advocated the Communism of wives, children and property among philosopher-kings and soldiers only to keep themselves free from personal worries.
5. **Moral Justice = Social Protection:** His justice is based on morality and not on facts, witness, judicial proceedings etc. It is far away from legality.
6. **Justice for Women = Sudra State of Mind State:** Plato was the first who thought for the women empowerment and established the justice for women by giving them equal rights in the state-affairs and armed forces.

7. **Educational Justice = Sant Philosophy:** He was the first to provide a state-controlled educational system for both-men and women so that the citizens should prepare themselves for the realisation and understanding of justice in the state.

Criticism

1. **Moral Justice:** His theory of justice is the concept of moral justice. He gives importance to duties rather than the rights. Rights and duties are the two sides of a coin so they should go simultaneously in the society.
2. **Centralisation of Power:** Plato has provided wide powers to the philosopher-king. He has not kept in his mind the human psychology that absolute power corrupts absolutely.
3. **Functional Specialisation:** Functional specialisation is itself the greatest obstacle in the all round growth and development of human personality.
4. He ignores the rights of human beings.
5. His justice with communism of wives, children and property ignores the human instincts and human psychology.
6. His concept of justice is not practicable and realisable.

Plato's Educational System = Dalit Philosophy

Plato has also given a plan for a state-controlled compulsory educational system in his book '***The Republic***'. Rousseau has remarked that the book is hardly a political work at all, but it is the Plato, education is a means of social righteousness and realisation of truth and not of social success.

Condition of Athens = Dr Bhagwan Das Ke Kitab on Dr B.R. Ambedkar's View

The condition of Athens compelled Plato to write about the educational system. During his time, the educational system was under private control of the Sophists. The Sophists were the group of teacher who came to Athens from other cities. They imparted instructions and knowledge only those who wished to learn. The Sophists charged heavy fees from them. Secondly, the Athenian Democracy was not efficient. The state was run by the selfish and corrupt statesmen. Thus, Plato gave the idea of the realisation of the Ideal State where the justice could be achieved only with the help of intellectual persons. Ernest Barker says, "it is an attempt to cure a mental malady by mental medicine."

Education in Ancient Greece

Education in Athens

The education in Athens was not in good condition. It was under the control of the Sophists. The state did not do anything for the education of the Athenians. Sophists and Isocrates were the two great schools prevailed in Athens. The sophists charged heavy fees for education. The females were deprived of education. The curriculum of Athenian education was divided into three stages—

- Primary stage = Childhood Ke Study
- Secondary stage = Adult Education
- Tertiary stage = Mature Knowledge

1. *Primary Stage:* Primary stage began 6 to 14 years. Athenian education was only for boys. Music and gymnastic were taught only boys at this stage. Music dealt with the knowledge of poetry, music, dance and other fine arts. Gymnastic included the physical training of the body.
2. *Secondary Stage:* A very few rich people had the privilege to get education in Athens at this stage because it was very costly affairs. Sophists and Isocrates took huge amount for providing higher education in Rhetoric and Politics. This stage began 14-18 years.
3. *Tertiary Stage:* The Athenian youth received military training in this stage for two years between 18-20 years. The state took the responsibility of military training only as the important part of education.

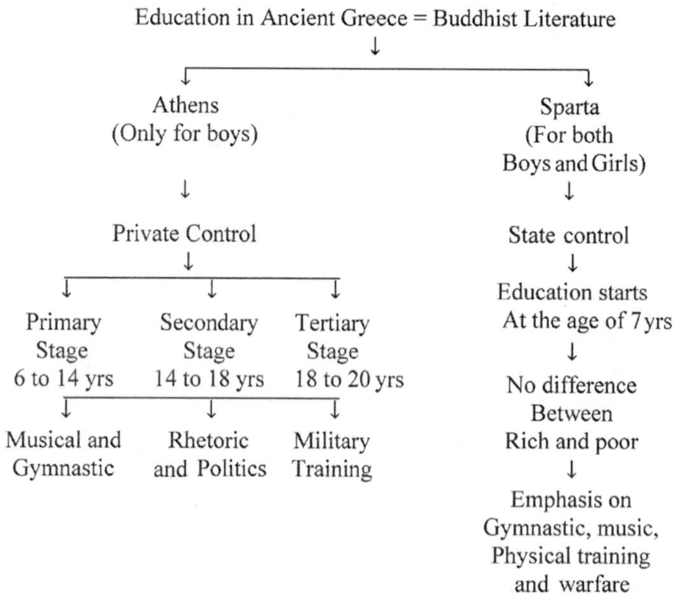

Education in Sparta

Spartan educational system was entirely different from Athens. Sparta was surrounded by different hostile states. There was continuous fear of attack on her. Thus, it was essential that the citizens should be trained in warfare to defend themselves. Taking this circumstance into consideration, the Spartan educational system was under the control of the state.

The state took the responsibility of education of its citizens. Both boy and girl children at the age of 7 yrs were separated from their parents and put in the hostels under the case of 'Perfects.' There was no discrimination between rich and poor. Emphasis was given to gymnastic, physical training and warfare so that they could face the crisis or foreign aggression etc. Music and choric-dancing = Natura Soul Ke view + G.B. Shaw Ke Kitab, were also taught to relax their body and revitalise their energy. In this way, Spartan educational system encouraged the feeling of patriotism and courage among citizens but no emphasis was given on wisdom.

Features of Plato's Education for Protection of Human Race = Sufi Ideology

Plato combined both the system of education prevailing in Athens and Sparta. The following are the important features of his education:

1. He planned for state controlled system of compulsory education.
2. It was meant for both boys and girls.
3. He divided his scheme of education into two parts.
   (a) Elementary education (6 to 20 years).
   (b) Higher education (20 to 35 years).
4. Military training was also compulsory for boys and girls.
5. Case for spiritual development was also taken into consideration so music was also kept in the curriculum.
6. Higher education consisted of 'dialectics'.
7. His education aimed at producing philosopher-kings.
8. There was strict censorship on all literature and artistic works so that young minds were not exposed to harmful ideas.

Platonic Concept of Education = Basic Knowledge

Plato has given a detailed curriculum for state controlled educational system. His educational system consists of two stages:

1. Elementary Education
2. Higher Education.

Elementary Education: It is further divided into three sub-stages:

- First sub-stage
- Second sub-stage
- Third sub-stage.

(a) First sub-stage: It was the childhood stage up to the age of six. The child was to be taught first simple religious truths and then moral truths like good manners, good tastes, love, hate, etc.

(b) **Second sub-stage:** In the second sub-stage of elementary education, from 6-18 years, knowledge of music and gymnastic should be given to both—boys and girls. Music and gymnastic are necessary for the development of soul, mind and physique. Music comprised of literature, poetry, singing, dancing writing and all other fine arts. Gymnastic included different exercises, diet and medicine.

(c) **Third sub-stage:** In this sub-stage of elementary education from 18-20 years, there was military training for both-boys and girls. It was compulsory in order to prepare them for the security and defence of the state. It aimed at the development of courage, self-control, character and discipline.

Those who did not want or qualify to join the higher education, they formed the second tier of the ruling class i.e. soldiers.

Higher Education for Philosopher-kings = Dr R.K. Gargotra Ke Soch: His higher education was meant for only to produce philosopher-kings. Those who showed their interests for further studies and aimed at becoming philosopher-kings, they opted for higher education. This stage is further divided into two sub-stages:

(a) **First sub-stage of Higher Education = Nam-theory: This sub-stage** began from 20 to 30 years. At the age of 20 years, an elimination test was conducted. The test qualified persons underwent another course of education for next 10 years. In this sub-stage, the men and women were given systematic scientific education including the study of Mathematics, Arithmetic, plane and Solid Geometry, Astronomy and Logic.

(b) **Second sub-stage of Higher Education = Brahmin Mat**: It began at the age of 30 years and ended at the age of 35 years. At the age of 30 years, another selective test conducted. The less qualified became the subordinate officers of the state and more qualified continued their studied for another five years. During these five years, they had to study mathematics and develop their power of Dialects. Dialects means to come at a conclusions after a long discussion and produce a proper definition. Dialectics is the instrument by which knowledge of the pure ideas is attained which gives us the higher reality. They became the philosopher-kings of the state = alit Ashoka King Ke Story.

Plato's Concept of Education (Curriculum)

1st Stage (6 yrs)	2nd Stage (6 to 18 yrs)	3rd Stage (18 to 20 yrs)	1st Stage (20-30 yrs)	2nd Stage (30-35 yrs)
Religion Truth, good Manners	Music And Gymnasti	Military Training	Mathematics Astronomy And logic	Dialectics

Practical Education = Work is Worship

At the age of 35 years, men and women became the philosopher-kings and occupied important positions of authority in the state. They were supported to deal with the problems of the administration for next 15 years. But their education never ended. It was a life-long process.

Criticism on Plato's Education = New Discovery

1. Plato's education has given a little attention towards the productive classes.
2. It is only for philosopher-kings.
3. It produces only academicians to rule over the state = Vedic Knowledge of the term Vid.
4. It does not make any effort for vocationalisation of education.
5. It overemphasises on philosophy of Negativism.
6. Censorship on literature is also one of the drawbacks of his education.
7. He does not pay any attention on individual differences.

Plato's Communism of Wives and Children = Sufi Dera

Plato designed his educational system in order to create the proper environment for the development of human mind and soul. He gives more importance to the philosopher-kings and soldiers because these classes represented reason and spirit and renounced the desires. He advocated the communism of wives children and property for them.

Plato had taken the idea of communism from his native state, Athens in which the state was considered the owner of all the forests and mines and the care-taker of individual property.

Communism of Wives and Children

Plato had developed the concept of communism of wives and children only for the philosopher-kings and soldiers in his own way. The following are the main points of his communism:

1. He has abolished marriage and children in the guardian class.
2. For him, family and property are the two sources of attachment which make the man selfish and corrupt.
3. Freedom from the bondage and responsibilities of the family make the guardians to follow their duties towards state dedicately.
4. For him, communism of wives means three things:
   (a) To prepare equal opportunities to women for their all round development
   (b) To provide them right to education
   (c) To set them free from the bondage of family.
5. He is in the favour of temporary marriage.
6. He abolished the institution of permanent marriage.
7. The children from temporary marriage are kept under the guidance of rest of the guardians so that they are considered as common children.
8. He is in the favour of birth of physically and mentally fit children in the state.

9. It is the duty of the state to bring up these children.
10. He advocates the concept of nationalisation of the family.

Criticisms

His communism of wives and children is criticised on the following grounds:

1. Aristotle has criticised Plato's communism of family as the family is a natural institution.
2. While giving the concept of communism of family, he destroys the foundation of morality which we learn from the family.
3. His communism of wives and children has deprived the guardians from the human natural instincts of belongingness.

Communism of Property = Lenin Ka Vichar

Plato has also explained the communism of property in his famous book "***The Republic***". He has not allowed any guardians to have any kind of property like a house, a treasure, gold and silver etc. The guardians are neither permitted to wear golden and silver ornaments nor to use golden and silver utensils. Their simple living and high thinking can defend their states. Otherwise they will become selfish and egoistic. They will never protect the state and solve internal conflicts.

Basic Principles of Communism of Property = Equality base knowledge

1. The first and the basic principle of Plato's communism property is that he considers the individual as a unit or part of the society. Thus, the individual feel happy and satisfy while performing his duties towards state.
2. For him, the justice will prevail in the state with the communism of property because the philosopher-kings should be selfless and without property in an ideal state. Only then, they can show wisdom and courage to do a lot for the state.

3. An ideal state can be realised only if the philosopher-kings are kept free from the bondage of marriage, children, family and personal property (Arondle Jonybee). It can be possible only through communism.
4. Moreover, he does not want to have a close relationship between political power and economic power. Plato allows only the general masses to have personal property in his ideal state. But this class is also controlled by the state.
5. The general masses or appetitive class can use it under the direction of the state.
6. The guardians depend on the appetitive class for fulfillment of their needs. In this way, Plato has distributed different functions to different classes in his ideal state for the maintenance of justice.

Criticism = Evolution of Mind

1. His communism of property is against the human psychology. It does not satisfy the natural instinct of possessiveness.
2. It leads towards political autocracy.
3. In actual practice, nobody can work hard for the growth of national income and in return, getting no economic benefits.
4. His communism of property means state's ownership over, property which is against individual liberty.
5. He has not justified the guardian class due to communism.
6. It is against the principles of liberty, equality, rights and even justice.
7. It destroys the institution of private property which is an important part of civilisation.

Plato's Ideal State = Gigit Agency

Plato was shocked at the death of his teacher Socrates. He realised that the state had no regards for such a pure soul and great philosopher. He imagined an Ideal State on the one of the important principles of his teacher, 'Beauty could exist without a beautiful thing.' Taking this idea into consideration, he made the sketches of his ideal state in his important work '***The Republic***' in the following ways:

1. **Well Planned Educational System = Modern Democracy Ka View:**
   (a) His educational system is under the control of the state.
   (b) He provides right to education to both boys and girls.
   (c) He also provides military education to both boys and girls.
   (d) There is a complete censorship on art and literature = Check on Brahminical Ideology.
2. **Division of the Society =Varna Education + Qutab Minor Ke Philosophy:** He has divided the society into three classes in his ideal state philosopher-kings, soldiers and peasants. Philosopher-kings are the rulers of the state. Soldiers perform their duties to protect the state internally and externally. The third and the lowest class is the Peasant class, consists of artisans, farmers and sculptors etc. They are concerned only with the production of consumable goods.
3. **Functional specialisation = Aar, Rambi Ke Kami:** his ideal state is based on functional specialisation of the citizen. Each individual performs his duty according to his capacity.
4. **Non-interference:** No individual is allowed to interfere in the matters of others. For Example, philosopher-kings are not supposed to interfere in the matters of soldiers or peasants.
5. **Communism of wives, children and property:** He has proposed the system of communism of wives, children and property in order to enable philosopher-kings and soldiers to give their best to the state.
6. **Philosopher-kings = Illiterate Samaj:** His ideal state should be run by the philosopher-kings who are the product of his educational system.
7. **Plato's Justice = new discovery of the term "wisdom" = Old Bible Ka view:** His ideal state aims at providing justice.

He is of the opinion that if the individuals belonging to the three classes in the state, perform their functions most efficiently and sincerely and without interference, there will be no class-struggle or conflict in the state. They will be selfless. Peace and prosperity will prevail in the state. Only then, justice can be established in the Ideal State.

Criticism

His ideal state has faced the following criticism:

1. His educational system is only for the producing philosopher-kings. It gives no stress on the third class i.e. peasant + Dalits.
2. His classification of the society into three classes has illogical basis.
3. He is failed to established relation between the politics and ethics.
4. His communism of wives and property is against the basic values of any human society. It is against the social norms as he advocates temporary marriages.
5. The philosopher-kings enjoy absolute power in his ideal state which may lead towards absolute corruption.
6. He has not explained the appointing authority of the rulers, the methods of punishment and the establishment of the laws.
7. It is against democratic values and encourages tyranny.
8. It is too idealistic to be practical = Sole-leather plants Ke dastana found in Muthi area of Jammu and Kashmir State = Watal History.

On the basis of criticism, his ideal state has identified him as the father of the Idealist school of thought. He has produced a Utopian concept. It is far away from realistic world.

Philosopher-kings = Raj-Rishi Ke Sabita

Plato has imagined an Ideal State which should be run by the philosopher-kings. For it, he has planned for a state controlled system of education which may give birth to philosopher-kings. They should be selected on the basis of their educational qualification ability and merit.

Characteristics of Philosopher-kings

1. **Product of Educational System:** Philosopher-kings are the product of lifelong his educational system. An individual can become a philosopher-king at the age of 35 and serve the state for next fifteen years i.e. 35-50 years.
2. **Importance to wisdom:** Plato gives importance to wisdom. Thus, his philosopher-kings represent wisdom and reason.
3. **Rule of Elite = Present Chamar Baradari:** The government in his ideal state is run by the elite. Only the intellectuals or an aristocracy of virtue should rule over the state.
4. **Absolute Powers:** His philosopher-kings enjoy absolute powers. They are not responsible to public opinion or bound by laws or customs.
5. **Communism of wives, children and property:** Plato prescribes communism of wives, children and property for the philosopher-kings. It means that they are not allowed to marry and have property. He prescribes only the temporary marriage for them to have best off-springs for the state. Moreover, he is of the opinion that his communism will help them to serve the state freely.
6. **Duties of the Philosopher-kings = Honest Approach:** Plato knows that absolute power in the hands of the philosopher-kings leads towards authoritarianism. Thus, he assigns the following duties for them which are laid down in the constitution of the state as rules:
   (i) The rulers should extend the state up to some limit under which the unity and self-sufficiency cannot maintain properly. The state should neither bigger nor smaller.
   (ii) In order to avoid conflict and instability in the state, the rulers should not encourage too much prosperity or

poverty because emergence of these two opposite classes leads towards instability.

(iii) It is the duty of the rulers to see that no citizen interferes in the performance of duties by the others.

(iv) He has not allowed them to bring any change in the educational system in the state.

Criticism

1. His philosopher-kings are the product of his educational system. Therefore, it produces academicians and not politicians. They do not have the knowledge of practical problems faced by the people.
2. The rule of philosopher-king is impracticable because it is very difficult to find a person having the complete knowledge of philosophy, mathematics, social life, psychology, law economics and political science.
3. He has not put any limit on the number of philosopher-kings.
4. It leads towards authoritarianism = Dalit-History.
5. He has not differentiated between philosophy and administration.
6. People have hard any contribution in state administration.
7. His communism also makes them corrupt = Political era from 1947 to onwards = Dalit Samaj found "pure" in nature.

Chapter - 3

Aristotle (384 B.C.-322 B.C.)

Aristotle, the father of Political Science, was born in 384 B.C. in Stagira, a city of Greece. His father, Nicomachus, was the court physician of Philip of Macedon. He was the greatest student of Plato who joined his famous Academy at the age of 17 years. He remained in his academy for 20 years as a student and a teacher. After the death of Plato in 347 B.C., Aristotle left the academy and began travelling. He went to Assos in Mysia and from there to Mitylene. Thus, he spent almost thirteen years visiting different parts of the world and studying different types of political institutions. In 342 B.C., he was called by the king Philip to look after the education of his son Alexander the great. He remained the tutor of Alexander for seven years. He returned to Athens and established his school "***Lyceum***". Since 335 B.C. till his death, he devoted himself to research, teaching and administrative duties in "***Lyceum***". Lyceum was more than in school or university. It was a public leisure centre, where Aristotle delivered his lectures to the selected students in the mornings and to the general public in the evenings. It was an informal school because there was no system of official enrollment, fees, syllabus, examination, degrees and technocrates.

He continued his studies in biology and history in his school. His students helped him to collect and compile research materials based on 158 constitutions. He had the largest collection of personal books and manuscripts. He had a library which was laid down the principles of library classification. Plato referred to Aristotle's home as "the house of the reader." After the death of Alexander, the anti-Macedonian party came in power. Thus, Aristotle left Athens for Euboea where he died in 322 B.C.

Important Works of Aristotle = Labour Concept

In the opinion of Zeller, Aristotle has written nearly 400 books. He was multi-dimensional philosopher. He wrote in the field of logic, ethics, metaphysics, politics, rhetoric, psychology and natural sciences. His important and matchless works can be classified into the following categories:

1. Logic	***Organon = Tao History Ka view.***
2. Ethics	***Nicomachean Ethics*** consists of 10 books. ***Eudemian Ethics.***
3. Metaphysics	***On Metaphysics*** included 14 books.
4. Politics	The Politics consists of 8 books, ***On the Constitution of Athens.***
5. Psychology	***On the Soul*** consists of 8 books. He also wrote small independent treaties on memory, dream etc.
6. Natural Sciences	***Physics*** consists of 8 books, ***Astronomy*** (4 books), ***Originand Decay*** (two Books); ***Meterology*** (4 books); ***Cosmology, Botany, History of Animals*** (10 books) etc.

Aristotle as the Father of Political Science

Aristotle was the student of Plato. He looked after the Academy after Plato's death. He learnt a lot from his teacher, Plato like

(i) Importance to education = Satsang.

(ii) Against democracy = Common view of Ambedkar's thought.

(iii) Justification of slavery = Qutab-ud-Din Albek Ke Story.

(iv) A good life could be possible in a city-state of a moderate state = Dalit race.

(v) State is not dispensable for the development of human faculties = Political Monger's lifestyle.

(vi) State exists for the moral development of the individuals = Dalit-King = Philosopher Raj-Rishi.

(vii) Importance to laws = New-History.

(viii) Close relationship between political and ethical problems.

(ix) Man is social by nature = Good human being.

(x) Bothe laid stress on check of population by birth control and destruction of unhealthy children = health problems + gas agency.

(xi) Bothe were conservative and believe their ideal as the city-state as the basis of their political thought.

(xii) Bothe believed in unity.

(xiii) There was no difference between state and society, for them = transport facilities of the modern time.

(xiv) Bothe gave man no right against the state.

(xv) Against trade and industry.

(xvi) Believed in aristocracy etc. = work and worship theory.

In spite of Plato's influence on Aristotle still Aristotle has his own political thought which makes a shift from political philosophy to political science. He never missed an opportunity to criticise his teacher, Plato. He was not the blind follower of his teacher. He learnt and implemented his master's teachings in his own way and developed his own thought. His practical approach made him the father of political science. It can be understood in the following ways:

1. **Study of Comparative Politics = Gandhi and Amloedkar:** Aristotle was the first to give the concept of comparative study. His theories were based on a detailed knowledge of the past history. He observed the things deeply, scientifically carefully and systematically. He conducted research on 158 constitutions of his time in which he had given a comparative study of the governments.

2. **Realistic Thinker = Sufi Kumba:** Aristotle emphasised on the problem of values and importance of ethical judgments.

He gave importance to the facts. For him, politics was the supremacy of ethics. He dealt with problem and came to the practical solution. Thus, he was the first realistic philosopher.

3. **Scientific Methodology:** His approach was scientific, empirical and descriptive. He was reformist.
4. **Importance to Laws**: Aristotle realised the importance of laws in the state. He established sovereignty of law in the state.
5. **Importance to Constitution**: Aristotle is the first who gives importance to the constitution also. For him, no constitution can exist without law. Moreover, the state is run by ruler with the consent of the people through constitutional law.
6. **Defining Democracy**: According to him, democracy is a form of government in which the poor are supreme. It is based on the principles of civic equality and freedom. The citizens have the equal right to share in the political affairs. The election to various offices should be based on universal suffrage.
7. **Organs of the Government**: He has also given three organs of the government i.e. deliberative, magistracy and judiciary.
8. **Separation of Ethics from Politics**: He separates ethics from the politics but he does not reject the ethical purpose of the state.
9. **Relationship between Politics and Economics**: He explains the conflict between haves and have nots. His classification of government differentiate between various types of oligarchy and democracy are based on economic issues. He is of the opinion that stability and prosperity in the state can be attained if there will be extremes of wealth and poverty.
10. **Nature of Man**: He is the first political thinker who remarks, "Man is a social and political animal." He lives in the society for the fulfill of his needs.
11. **Nature of State**: He is of the opinion that family is the smallest union and unions of number of families constitute a village. And numbers of villages constitute a state.

12. **Classification of the Government**: He is the first who has classified the government into six types. Three are pure forms i.e. monarchy, aristocracy and polity; on the other hand, three corrupt forms of government consist of tyranny, oligarchy and democracy.
13. **Defining Revolution**: He has also defined the concept of revolution and its different causes. At the same time, he has also given its remedies.
14. He gives importance to the public opinion.
15. He is also considered as the father of modern conservatives because he emphasises on the preservation of the existing institutions.
16. He is the first to stress on the principle of maximum happiness of the maximum number of the people.

Aristotle's View on Household = Elevated Soul

Aristotle gives importance to household in his political philosophy which fulfils the basic and important functions of the individual. His household consists of family, women, children, property and slaves.

Family: Women, Children and Private Property = Russian Revolution Ka View of 1917 + Peasant Movement of India

Aristotle gives importance to family life which is based on love and friendship.

1. He considers family as the first natural institution arising out of the union of male and female on the one hand and the master and slave on the other.
2. He gives importance to man as the master of his house, his family and property.
3. He has to control the household affairs in three different ways:
   (a) As a husband over his wife
   (b) As a parent over his children
   (c) As a master over his slaves

4. Every household is a part of a polis.
5. He has given 18 to 37 years as the marriageable age for men and women.

Private Property = Pandava Race

Aristotle is the first who holds that the discipline of the family life can be maintained with the help of institution of private property. According to him, "Property, in the sense of a bare livelihood, seems to be given by nature herself to all, when they are grown up." He justifies the private property as a gift of nature. It is the most essential part of social economy and for household affairs. The following are his important arguments about private property:

1. Aristotle is the strong support of private property. He is of the opinion that property is an important instrument to lead a good life.
2. It is the great source of personality development.
3. Each citizen should have two kinds of property one near the border and other near the city.
4. He differentiates between the natural and unnatural acquisition of property. The acquisition of wealth from land-crops or animals is the natural property. On the other hand, the wealth by the exchange of commodities for profit is unnatural.
5. He is not in the favour of interest-oriented property.
6. For him, agriculture is the best natural function of the citizens.
7. In this way, he prefers landed property to trade and commerce. He wants the circulation of the right amount of wealth in the state.
8. He stresses on the certain economic activities like fishing, shoemaking and farming.
9. Through these economic activities, the producer and his family directly get benefit and fulfill their needs.
10. He advocates the continuance of the fixed amount of property for generation.

11. For it, he has fixed the number of the children. Thus, he gives the concept of birth control.
12. Private property should not bring a disparity in the state, so he has a definite leaning in the favour of common meal system.

Criticism of Aristotle on Plato's concept of communism = Dalit-Samaj

Aristotle has never missed the chance to criticise his teacher, Plato even in his communism also. Plato wants to bring and maintain unity and harmony in the state through the means of communism of wives, children and property. Aristotle criticises him by giving the following arguments:

1. The unity and harmony can be maintained in the state through proper education for the individuals.
2. The ownership of private property and family is a natural right of the individual. Thus, it is very important for the personality development of the individuals.
3. Aristotle has also rejected the Platonic concept of common ownership of property because common ownership is the source of disputes.
4. For Aristotle, private property is an important source of happiness for the individuals so the Platonic communism can never bring happiness in the state.
5. Communism of property destroys the sentiments of charity and social services. For that, one needs property.

Similarly, he criticises Plato's communism of wives and children in the following ways:

1. Aristotle thinks that a woman cannot be a wife of all guardians. It will create conflict in the society and destroy all harmony. Moreover, the society will be polluted.
2. Children in this system will be badly neglected. Nobody will take the care of these children. The institution of love affection and sentiments will be destroyed.

3. Everyone's responsibility will actually be no body's responsibility. In other words, the responsibility can be shifted to one-another.
4. The dignity of women can always be in danger.
5. It is against the laws of nature.
6. There are more chances of all kinds of corruption.

Aristotle's Concept of Slavery = Chamar thought or Slave Dynasty of India

For Aristotle, State is made up of households in which the slaves are the important parts of household affairs and management so slaves are the living possessions of household.

His Justification of Slavery + Good Human Souls

1. **Slavery as a Natural Institution:** For him, slavery is a natural institution because all are not equal by nature so the governing souls should rule over the others. In other words, the superior should rule over inferior.
2. **Necessary Instrument:** Slaves are the necessary instruments of action. A slave is a living possession without reason. He cannot do anything by applying his brain. He needs the directions and guidance of his master. He acts according to the commands of his master.
3. **Useful for both = Dr Shabnam Grewal + Razia Sultana:** For him, slavery is useful for both the master and slave. A slave's association with his master feels himself as a pride because the slave enables him to attain virtue and wisdom; and provides leisure to him (master). It is sort of certain kind of mentally and intellectual satisfaction, he provides to him.
4. **Family Security = IPS Officer:** Slavery is necessary for the security of family and society. Each natural household requires slaves for the proper management of household affairs.
5. **Necessary for Welfare State = New Education System:** Slave also play important role for the progress and prosperity of the state. The citizens find the leisure only due to slaves

so that they can effectively and efficiently look after the management of the state.

6. **Best conditions for Slaves = Kacha Houses to Pacca Houses:** Aristotle has justified the slavery on the ground that the slaves are provided the best conditions by their masters.
7. **Slavery is the Necessity for the Realisation of God:** According to Aristotle, the slavery is the necessity for the masters to lead good life so they need slaves.
8. **Friendly Behaviour = Dalit Scholar Ka View:** The master should have a friendly behaviour with his slave. He should not misuse his power.
9. **Chance of Emancipation = Re-written history:** The slaves have a chance of emancipation if they develop their reason and capacity for self-direction.

Qualification for Slave = Neglected Samaj + Sudra concept

1. Aristotle favours the enslavement of only those persons who are mentally deficient.
2. He is not in the favour of enslaving prisoners of war.
3. He is against the force able conversion of prisoners of war as slaves.
4. Masters cannot treat them with cruelty. Otherwise, they will be punished by the state.
5. For him, a Greek should not enslave a Greek except only casually.
6. Only persons of other races, which are inferior to the Hellenes, should be slaves.
7. Intellectually inferior to prisoners of war should be enslave.

Criticisms

1. His justification of slavery is against the modern notion of equality, rights and liberty.
2. His classification of superior and inferior is unjustified.
3. His view on slavery is based on racial prejudice.

4. He has no fixed any criteria for the classification whether a person belongs to the superior class or the inferior class.
5. He considers slavery as a hereditary institution.
6. His theory of slavery creates confusion.
7. Slaves are not the property like land, house etc.
8. It is also against the notion of modern justice.

Aristotle's Classification of Government

Aristotle has conducted research on 158 constitutions of city-states. For him, there is no different among state, government and constitution. For him, the character of the state is determined by the 'constitution.' Any change in the constitution brings the change in the identity of the state = V.K. Puri + Sunita Puri Ke Kitab + Ghai Family Ke International Politics.

Basic of the Government = Chura Concept

The government in a state can be constituted on three basis:

(a) Birth (b) Wealth (c) Number

Aristotle classifies government on the basis of number to hold sovereign power i.e. quantitative and qualitative basis.

Forms of Government

Quantity base	*Quality base*	
	Pure form	***Corrupt form***
One	Monarchy (supreme virtue)	Tyranny (force, descent, selfishness)
Few	Aristocracy (mixture of virtue and wealth)	Oligarchy (greed for wealth and selfishness)
Many	Polity Martial and muscular virtues, power residing with the middle class poor people.	Democracy (equality with power in the hands of the poor).

Aristotle has given six types of the governments three are the pure forms of governments—Monarchy, Aristocracy and Polity. On the other hand, Tyranny, Oligarchy and Democracy are three corrupt forms of the governments. For him, if the government takes into the consideration the welfare of all, it is the pure form of government. Contrary to it, if the government serves the private and selfish interests of the ruling class, it becomes a corrupt or perverted form of government.

He explains monarchy as a rule of one man. The government is run by hereditary succession with supreme virtue for common good and tyranny is its corrupt form which is based on force, cruelty and selfishness. Aristocracy is the rule of few persons representing the mixture of virtue and wealth. It works for the welfare of the people. Oligarchy is the corrupt form if few greedy and selfish people. Polity is the government of all, for the good of all. It represents martial and muscular virtues. Its perverted form is Democracy.

Cycle of Change through Guru Siksha

Aristotle is of the opinion that the form of government is not permanent. It keeps on changing in a circle. Monarchy can be changed into Tyranny. Similarly Aristocracy is replaced by Oligarchy and Polity by Democracy. He calls this process of change as 'cycle of change.'

Criticism

1. He has given only six types of government. It does not cover a number of other governments like parliamentary and presidential forms of government, limited monarchy, federal, unitary, totalitarian regimes etc.
2. He keeps the democracy in the category of corrupt form of government but in the contemporary world, democracy is the best form of government.
3. It is wrong to say that Democracy is the Government of the poor people. Democracy is successfully functioning in the richest countries like America.
4. He has not differentiated among the state, government and the constitution.
5. His classification is not based on any scientific principles.

Aristotle's Views on Revolution = Recovery of Old History in New Form

The political instability in the Greek city-states made Aristotle to think about the revolution, its causes and remedies.

Meaning of Revolution = Advance View Found in "History"

Aristotle has defined revolution as:

1. Major or minor change in the constitution of the state = '*A Primitive History of the Dalit Samaj*'.
2. The constitution remains unchanged but the political power may change.
3. Change in the form of government e.g. overthrow of oligarchy by democracy.
4. Change in the institution or set of person.

Causes of Revolution = Religious Propaganda

Aristotle gives the two important causes of revolution in the State:

- General causes = Classless society.
- Specific causes = par excellence.

I. **General Causes = Classless Society**

   1. Inequality is the most general cause of revolution.
   2. Demand for social, political and economic equality.
   3. Undue importance to some people.
   4. Carelessness in public appointments.
   5. Misuse of authority by the disloyal and corrupt persons.
   6. Psychological causes such as love of gain and honour, fear, insolence etc.
   7. Neglect the minor change.
   8. Political differences.
   9. Free flow of immigrants.
   10. Election intrigues.
   11. Concentration of power = Natural King.

12. Rivalry among the members of different races living in a state.
13. The victory of one nation by another nation.
14. Disproportionate increase of any part etc.

II. Specific Causes of Revolution = par excellence

He explains the specific causes of revolution in the context of different form of government:

1. **Monarchy:** Revolution takes place in monarchy only because of cruel behaviour of the king or his undignified rule. Moreover, fear, terror and injustice are also certain causes of revolution.
2. **Aristocracy:** Revolutions in Aristocracy arise due to the jealousy.
3. **Polity:** The extreme mixture of democratic and oligarchic elements gives birth to a revolution in the polity.
4. **Tyranny:** A feeling of hatredness for ruler in the minds of people leads towards revolution in tyranny = Brahminical propaganda.
5. **Oligarchy:** Revolution occurs in Oligarchy either due to rivalry or oppressive and dictatorial nature of the rule.
6. **Democracy:** Revolutions are caused due to the excessive use of powers.

Prevention of Revolution = Administrative Measures

Aristotle has suggested the following measures to avoid a revolution in the state:

1. An effort should be made to develop a friendly atmosphere.
2. All offices should be open to all on the merit-basis.
3. There should be no monopoly of few families in the offices.
4. Political power should be decentralised.
5. Foreigners and strangers should be kept away from the important political offices.
6. Mal-practices and bribery should be avoided.

7. The rule should keep an eye on the small changes in the society so that the beginning of a revolt should be nipped in the bud.
8. No person in the state should be allowed to rise suddenly. It means that slow and gradual promotions should be applied in the state.
9. Loyalty towards constitution, administrative capacity and integrity of character should be the criteria for the highest offices in the state.
10. Transparency is essential in the financial matters in order to gain popularity and political stability.
11. The changes in the distributions of wealth should be checked.
12. The ruler should be popular with the help of sound defence against foreign attack.
13. The feeling of patriotism should be promoted.
14. The ruler should respect the property, rights and dignity of the people.
15. The ruler should participate in the public worship and religious ceremonies of the people.
16. Chopping off the heads of the inconvenient powerful leaders etc.

Aristotle's Best Practicable State = Pigeon hole Karma

Concept and Characteristics = *Main Features of the Indian Constitution*

Aristotle thinks for an Ideal State which is the best form of government but it cannot be practicable. Thus, he gives a detailed account of the best practicable state i.e. The Polity. For him, Polity is that kind of government which avoids the extremes of oligarchy and democracy. It is also known as the ***"Constitutional Government" =Dr B.R. Ambedkar Ka Vichar.*** He uses this word 'Polity' in two different ways:

1. Polity means the constitution, any kind of constitution whether in aristocracy, monarchy, oligarchy or democracy is "Polity".

2. He uses 'Polity' for constitutional government. Later on, it stands for mixture of Oligarchic and democratic elements by avoiding their extreme sides.

In oligarchy, very few rich persons rule over many poor persons for the protection of their class interest. Concentrating the power and ownership of private property in the hands of few make this class dominant and oppressive.

In Democracy, many poor persons dominate in the affairs of the state. It is based on the principles of freedom and equality. Equality is obtained through equal right to participate in the political affairs of the government. Everyone has an opportunity of ruling and to be ruled.

Thus, he avoids both the extreme richness and extreme poverty and asserts that the power in the best practicable state should lie in the middle class.

Characteristics of Best-Practicable States = par excellence theory

According to Aristotle, society is divided into two classes—the rich and the poor. Only a middle class can maintain a balance in the state. The following are some of the important characteristics of his best-practicable state of middle-class:

1. Extreme richness gives birth to arrogance and disobedience to authority because the rich know how to rule but do not know how to be ruled.
2. Extreme poverty leads to complete control of the people so they know how to be ruled. They are unable to understand how to rule.
3. Only the middle class knows how to rule and how to be ruled in turn because it is neither rich nor poor.
4. The best-practicable state comprises of the middle-class which is in the majority.
5. There are greater chances of the stable government in a middle-class dominant society.

6. Moreover, there are less chances of revolution or revolt in the middle-class dominant society.
7. The middle class in polity provides a popular government and avoids the evils of mob-rule.
8. It maintains a balance between the principles of wealth and number.
9. It gives a mixed constitution of combination of elements of Oligarchy and democracy.
10. It is the most stable, durable and well-administered practicable state under the control of the middle-class.

To conclude, though Maxey states, "On theoretical grounds, the validity of this thesis may be easy to dispute—middle-class mediocrity is no shining ideal for the foundation of a state." But the historical records shows that most of the stable, durable and well-administered political societies have been controlled by the middle class people. Aristotle's best practicable state run by middle class is applicable even in the modern states = Jammu and Kashmir Ke Darti.

Chapter - 4

Machiavelli (1469-1527 A.D.) = Princely State Ka Idea

The father of modern political science, Niccolo Machiavelli was born on 3rd May, 1469 at Florence in Italy. His father Bernardo was a civil lawyer. After completing his education at the University of Florence, he joined the Florentine diplomatic service. At the age of 29, he became the secretary to the second chancery with responsibilities in foreign affairs diplomatic, administrative and military in nature. His humanistic training made him a hardworking, patriotic and honest public functionary.

"*Machiavelli was very much fond of history*". He established his own library at home where he read those good books that dealt with life's experience. He met the prominent statesmen of his day like Julius II (the most important Renaissance Pope), Emperor Maximilian I of Germany, King Louis XII of France and Cardinal Cesare Borgia. It was Borgia who became the source of inspiration to Machiavelli to write ***"The Prince" about Jammu and Kashmir State.*** He quoted in his important work ***"The Prince"*** for Borgia's ruthless and daring leadership and role of fortune = Karma Theory + Dandniti of Raj-Rishi scholar.

He visited the court of Louis XII on a diplomatic assignment for six months in July 1500 where he realised the critical condition of his state Florence i.e. unstable republican government run by the merchants who did not want to spend money on the military. He himself was insulted and referred as 'Mr Nothing.' He got the key to success in politics was to be clever, thrifty, cultured, forceful, decisive and ruthless. He reflected all these qualities of a ruler in his important work "***The Prince of Wale College" and G.G.M. Science College Ke Construction.***

When the Republic of Florence collapsed in 1512, he faced a lot of crisis. He was dismissed, tortured and imprisoned. But he granted amnesty with the ascendancy of the new rulers, the Medici family. As a token of gratitude, he dedicated "***The Prince***" to the Medici family. He spent his time by reading history, understanding statecraft, non-philosophical texts etc. after his releasing from imprisonment. In 1520, he was commissioned by the University of Florence to write a chronicle and the annals of Florence, which was published as the "***History of Florence***" in 1525. He died on June 22,1527.

Renaissance and Its Impact on Machiavelli = Labour Class

The word Renaissance stands for the revival of ancient values and culture, the Greek and Roman ideas and notions which the Christianity had suppressed in the medieval era. The Renaissance signifies a rebirth of the human soul in order to achieve liberty, self-confidence and optimism. It focuses on the Greek ideal of the goodness of the person, the beauty and glory of the earth, the joy of existence, the insignificance of the supernatural and the importance of the supernatural and the importance of the present. Renaissance is the period where the medieval era ends and modern era begins.

Italy was the homeland of Renaissance. As Laski observes, "The whole of the Renaissance is in Machiavelli."

Impact on Machiavelli = Dalit-Samaj Ke Soch

Historical Background = Basic View

Machiavelli saw the division of Italy into five groups i.e. Kingdom of Naples, Territory of Roman Catholic Church, the Duchy of Milan, the Republic of Venice and the Republic of Florence. They had warfare with each other. Moreover, there was a serious threat to their existence clue to the strong states like France and Spain. He wanted to unite these five states under an absolute monarch.

1. **Condition of Italy = Old Concept into New Form**
   (i) Politics was not based on good Christian ethics but on selfish interests.
   (ii) The Italian society was suffered from political corruption and moral degeneration.
   (iii) The government did not bother about injustice cruelty and murder.
   (iv) Force and craft were the master-keys to success.
   (v) There was problem of lawlessness and selfishness and corruption.
2. **Influence of Aristotle = Working Class Ke Halit:** Machiavelli was very much influence by Aristotle. He found the solution from the ancient learning. He learnt the following ideas from Aristotle:
   (i) Separation of ethics from politics.
   (ii) State is the highest organisation of human beings.
   (iii) Three-fold division of the states i.e. Monarchy, aristocracy and democracy.
   (iv) Historical method.
3. **Influence of Marsiglio = Radha Soami Mission Ke Teaching:** He borrowed me idea of secularism and the political utility of religion from Marsiglio.
4. **Importance to History = Recongnisation of the author:** He had very practical approach towards history. He was of the opinion that the people should read and learn the lives and experience of great men of the past. Their experience will prove useful and helpful for understanding the present.

The contemporary situation and the Renaissance movement influenced Machiavelli. He broke the medieval thought and gave new and modern political thought in his important works. ***"The Prince and The discourses".*** His writings awakened in human beings a new consciousness and new values of life. He gave a new political thought about the human nature, human motives, qualities of the prince, separation of ethics from politics, secular and sovereign state, power politics, national army etc. thus, he was the creator of this Renaissance which dominated Italy in general and Florence in particular. He was on the border line between the medieval and modern ages. He set free the political thought from the chains of the religion.

Machiavelli's Views on Human Pschyology

Nature and Motives = *Changing View of "History" = Dalit Samaj Ke Kitab*

Machiavelli has borrowed the idea of man as a social animal from Aristotle. But he gave a very dark picture of human nature. He compared human nature with animal nature. He explained human nature in his important work ***The Prince*** in the following ways:

1. **Selfish and Self-centred:** Man is selfish and self-centred. He always cares for himself and his selfish interest. He is greedy and sensual creature.
2. **Aggressive by Nature:** Man is aggressive by nature. He shows interest to acquire more and more. He has always conflict with others so he is surrounded by anarchy.
3. **Wicked**: Human beings are always wicked in nature. They always work against the collective interests if there is clash of their own interest with the collective interests.
4. **Timid:** Human beings are always timid, fearful and coward. The man never wants to resist and finds the easiest way to follow the established norms of the society.
5. **Weak:** He is fundamentally weak, ungrateful, artificial. He avoids the danger but desires to gain maximum.
6. **Acquisitive:** He is of the opinion that man loves private property so, he would ready to murder his father. He is very much fond of the benefits and rewards.
7. **Dissatisfaction:** Every human being always remains dissatisfied in the society. He wants more and more power.
8. **Stupid and Irrational:** Human beings are stupid and irrational in nature. They play tricks with others and misguide others.

9. **Desire for Novelty:** Machiavelli observes that human beings have desire of novelty, change and love.
10. **Ambitious:** Man is ambitious by nature. When he remains dissatisfied, he fulfills his desires through war etc.
11. **Egoistic:** He is egoistic in nature = modern Gujjar Samaj = Brahmin Mat.
12. **Lack of Honest:** He is dishonest by nature.
13. **Love for Power:** He loves to remain in power so that others obey him.
14. **Desire for Freedom:** He loves freedom for himself and not for others.
15. **Glorify the Past = Rig-Veda Ke History + Four Vedas:** Machiavelli points out that human mind tends to glorify the past, dissatisfy with the present and hope for a better future.

Motivations = Mature Culture

Machiavelli has given the following implication for the motivation of human nature:

1. **State Control = no history of the upper class:** Machiavelli is of the opinion that the state has to check the wicked nature of human beings who are selfish. The state should use maximum force for it.
2. **Absolute Power = Dalit King Ke Story:** He has given the concept of absolute power. He gives absolute power to the Prince. The Prince should rule the state with absolute power without caring his wicked, selfish, and egoistic and dishonesty people. The Prince advises to avoid the morality.

Criticism

His ideas about human nature can be criticised on the following grounds:

1. Human beings are not always selfish, egoistic, wicked, coward, aggressive in nature.
2. He has given only the dark picture of human beings.
3. Human beings are the mixture of good and bad elements.

4. He has not given any scientific reason about human nature why they are so.
5. It establishes that fear, and not the will of people is the basis of the state.
6. How long a ruthless and forceful state exists?

Machiavelli's Views on Relationship between Ethics and Politics = New Discovery

Medieval political thinkers considered religion as the basis of the state. State is one of the parts of the religion or the church. Machiavelli rejected this ideology. He separated ethics from politics. He argued that religion was subordinate to the state. For him, religion is the rule of conduct of the individual. It is his personal affairs. On the other hand, politics is the rule of conduct of the state.

He was anti-church but not anti-religion. He gave importance to religion in man's social life. At the same time, religion also played a significant role for the health and prosperity of the state. It was an indispensable part of the civic life so the princes and the rulers were to use religion in strengthening their power effectively and carefully.

Machiavelli proposed two types of conceptions of ethics:

(a) One for the public (ruler)

(b) Other for the private (citizens)

Public Ethics = Indiscipline Among Upper Class Society: For him, the public ethics or morality was very important for the stability of the state. It was directly linked with the religion and liberty so in order to remain in power, he advised the prince to take the advantage from the religion. If the ruler was not religious or had very little faith in it, he would develop the belief in religion. In this way, he considered religion as a coercive force. He gave importance to classical qualities like war, courage, intelligence, fame and strength, ambition, vitality, self-assertiveness, virtue etc. He also criticized Christianity which made the people charitable and weak, glorifying qualities like renunciation, lowliness other-worldliness, patience under injustice.

He defined civic religion as based on fear and respect for authority and produce courageous and brave men for state.

In this way, public ethics aimed at keeping and increasing the power of the ruler. The ruler as the creator of the state was not only outside the law, but he was outside the morality also because in order to remain in power, he was permitted the use of immoral means like fraud, forgery, trickery, violence, breach of faith, murder etc. At the same time, Machiavelli condemned for open advocacy of immorality in the public life. Thus, as Sabine and Dunning remark that Machiavelli was neither moral nor immoral but unmoral in politics.

Criticism

1. His views on ethics and politics misguide the politicians and permit them to commit all sorts of crimes in the name of security and integrity of the state.
2. It is impossible to say that public and private interests are same.
3. His theory of "end justifies the means" goes directly against Mahatma Gandhi's theory of "means justifies the end."
4. It can be possibility that the ruler can identify his personal and selfish interests with the national interest.

Preservation and Extension of State Power = Coming Election of the J and K State

Machiavelli considers the state as the highest association to which the citizens must surrender themselves. He defines state as an organised force for the maintenance and security of the people. He discusses the nature of state in the following ways:

1. He believes in secular state.
2. He should provide security to person and his property.
3. A state has to expand its territory and power.
4. A well-ordered, strong and stable government should be at the centre.
5. It should consider its neighbours as the real or powerful enemies.

6. Thus, it should have citizen army or national army. The national army is also essential for stability of the government.
7. An army should consist of its own citizens between the ages of 17 and 40. They should be physically well-trained in arms and military skills.
8. State should be run by a single person and he should create the laws which reflect the national character of the state.
9. He considers the Republican state as the best, but under them prevailing conditions, he favoured Monarchy and completely avoided Aristocracy.
10. He gives importance to law in his state. He believes in good laws are the foundation stones of the state.

He classifies the nature of state in two different circumstances:

1. Normal State
2. Perverted state or at the time of Crisis.

1. **Normal State = J and K Ke History:** According to him, the normal state is the one in which the citizens are faithful and law-obeying. They have the spirit of patriotism. They ready to serve their motherland at all costs. Here, a normal state has a tendency to grow and expand, it becomes self-sufficient.
2. **Perverted State = Dr Farooq + Mehbooba Ke Politics**: On the other hand, the state cannot grow and expand at the time of crisis. Here, Machiavelli has given certain following suggestions to the prince or ruler for the preservation and extension of the state power:
   (i) **Use of Power Ruthlessly = Security Force Ka Danda:** The Prince should not hesitate to use power ruthlessly against those who challenge his authority. He should mercilessly crush all opposition by execution and bloodshed.
   (ii) **Fox and Lion = Dalit Historian:** A good Prince should be cunning as fox and as brave as lion.

(iii) **Believe in Peace and Calmness:** He should try to maintain peace and calmness in the state so that people can live a comfortable life.

(iv) **Exploit Ethics, Moral and Religious Values:** A good prince should usefully exploit the moral feeling and sentiments of the people.

(v) **Strong Decision Maker = Dalit-Philosopher King:** A Prince should take strong and final and quick decisions. He should not even hesitate to declare a war.

(vi) **Strong National Army=Dalit Samaj:** The Prince should have strong national army for the survival of the state.

(vii) **Prince as a Good Soldier and Commander:** The Prince should know the art of war. He should be a good soldier and commander in the battle-field.

(viii) **Patriotism and Sense of Duty = Dalit Samaj:** He should be patriot and inculcate the feeling of patriotism and sense of duty in himself and his subjects.

(ix) **Violate his Promises = Standby Story + Dr B. R. Ambedkar Ji Ka View**: Machiavelli is of the view that the prince can have the right to violate his promises for the interests, security, unity and integrity of the state. The Prince should not taken into consideration of just or unjust, pitiful or cruel, honourable or dishonourable.

(x) **Popular among People = Humanity Base Knowledge:** He should try to become popular among people and try to win the sympathy and co-operation of the people.

(xi) **Fear among People:** He should create such an atmosphere where people have a feeling of fear and not hated.

(xii) **Dishonesty and Fraud = BJP and Congress Government**: He should be dishonest and fraud person in order to preserve the state.

(xii) **Refrain from Wealth and Women = Sufi Ideology:** A successful prince should keep himself away from the wealth, property and women of his subjects. Otherwise, he has to face the result in the form of revolt etc. because the people are very sensitive about these.

(xiii) **Secrecy = Barani Pul Ka Dera:** He should maintain secrecy and keep an eye on any kind of leakage of plan or information.

(xiv) **Neither Friends nor Foes = No friendship, no enemity:** A Prince must realise that state neither has friends nor foes. He should take advantages from the favourable opportunity.

(xv) **Education as an Instrument of Propaganda = Upper Class Society:** The Prince should use education as a selfish instrument of propaganda. Though educational curriculum, people can feel that their interests are identical with those of the Prince.

(xvi) **Avoid Self-Praise = Dalit-King Ke Dastana:** The Prince should avoid self-praise, flattery, sycophants etc. so that he can decide the matters independently.

(xvii) **Destroy the Freedom of People = Controlling System of the Dalit-King:** When a Prince conquers the territory of another state, he should destroy the freedom of the people because they accustom to freedom, can never reconcile to the loss of the same.

(xviii) **Show Off = Brahmin + Megh Samaj:** He should try to show himself as good, sincere, humane and sympathetic person.

(xix) **Keep a Distance = Dignity of the Scholar:** He should keep a distance with the general masses. He should not listen everybody. He should have some selective and intelligent counsellors and listen them patiently.

(xx) **Financial Matters = No Problem:** The Prince should know the public opinion about the financial matters of the state so that he can get the public support and co-operation.

(xxi) **Knowledge about the Strength of the Enemy = Zero Lebel Ke Study:** He should know about the strength of the enemy. He should neither under-estimate nor over-estimates the strength of the enemy. He should destroy him in his initial stage.

(xxii) **No Place for Friends in Politics:** He should make his friends realise that their co-operation is the base for the continuation of friendship. He should not have permanent friend because a friend of today can be an enemy of tomorrow.

(xxiii) **Aim at Expansionism:** He should aim at expansion of the territory of the state.

Criticism = New View Point = Dalit-i-illahi Liberation Front

His theory of preservation and extension of state can be criticised on the following grounds:

1. Sabine argues that he has been represented as an utter cynic, an impassioned patriot and ardent nationalist.
2. He attacks undue importance to force for unity the people.
3. He explains in detail the role of the ruler as law-giver, in molding the moral, religious and economic life of the people.
4. He fails to understand that the prince as human being may try to promote his selfish interests at the cost of the public as well as national interest.

Chapter - 5

John Stuart Mill (1806-1873)= Untouchable History of the Art Historian

John Stuart Mill was the most eminent influential and popular political thinker of the nineteenth century. He was born on 20th May, 1806 in London. His father James Mill came from Scotland and began with journalism as his career. He devoted his time on writing "*A History of British India*" which he completed in eleven years = A Modern History the Untouchable (1707 to Present Day).

J.S. Mill was influenced by India through the writings of his father. He was a brilliant boy. He began the study of Greek at the age of four years, Latin, History and Classics at the age of eight. At the age of 11, he started to help his father by proof-readings of his father's books. At the age of 13, he deeply studied the writings of the English classical economists and published an introductory text-book in economics entitled "*Elements of Political Economy*" = Old Dogra State, in 1820 at the age of 14 years. He was very much fond of poetry and art so he read the important works of Thomas Carlyle, Samuel Taylor Coleridge, Comte Goethe and William Wordsworth. He also reviewed Alexis de Tocqueville's book "*Democracy in America*" in two parts in 1835 and 1840.

He began to write for newspapers and periodicals at the age of 20 years. He started his political philosophy with "*System of Logic*". "*On Liberty and the Subjection of Women*" were related to important issues of rights, liberty, law etc. He gave an ideal government based on proportional representation, protection of minorities and institution of self-government in his important and famous book "*The Considerations on Representative Government*". He wrote a number of books, pamphlets and articles such as "*Enfranchisement of Women, Dissertation and Discussions*", "*Thoughts of Parliamentary Reforms*", "*Consideration on Representative Government, Utilitarianism, Women Suffrage, and Three Essays on Religion etc.*

He also worked under the East India Company in 1823 as a clerk and became the head of the department in 1856. He continued his post till 1858 at the end of the company rule in India. He died on 8th May, 1873 at Avignon in England.

J.S. Mill's Views on Liberty after Kashmir Issue

J.S. Mill is a great champion of the individual liberty. He has developed his concept of liberty in his important work "*Essays on Liberty*". He gives a complete and systematic philosophy of individual liberty originated from the latin term Libertas.

According to him, "Liberty consists in doing what one desires and does not desire to fall into the river = Life is stream."

He is in the favour of individual liberty in two senses:

1. **Negative sense = No Insaniyat:** In its negative sense, the society has no right to interfere in the matters of individual. It means that he promotes laissez-faire and individualism. In this way, the state should not have any kind of interfere in the affairs of the individual. Liberty is the sovereignty of the individual over himself.
2. **Positive Sense = Insaniyat Ka Vichar:** In its positive sense, it stands for the grants of the largest and the greatest amount of freedom for all round development of the individual.

On the basis of these two senses, he supports the negative liberty.

Negative Liberty = No politics + capability: It consists of inward dominance of conscience, liberty of thought and expression, absolute freedom of opinion and sentiment of all subjects, scientific, moral, theology, practical or speculative etc.

Liberty of Thought and Expression = *Dalit Issue*

While stressing on liberty of thought and expression, he argues that the state has no right to suppress the independent thinking of an individual because the truth develops after a detailed discussions. He states that history is witness to it. Some opinions were not tolerated by the authorities in the past, are now recognised as the best. He gives the example of the execution of Socrates and Jesus Christ = Chura History.

Thus, he has a very defensive attitude towards freedom of thought and expression. He is of the opinion that freedom of thought and expression proves helpful in creativity also. And creativity can be effective only if it allows to function properly and freely. It helps in the development of a humane, civilised and moral person. But customs, conventions and mass opinion are the greatest obstacles in the way of freedom of thought and expression. He is against these kinds of outdated customs and practices which are not based on reason.

He believes in individuality. For him, it means the power or capacity for critical enquiry and responsible thought, self-development and expression of free-will. He supports absolute liberty of conscience, belief and expression for human development.

Role of Education: Nam-Theory: He is of the opinion that education plays an important role for developing intellectual and critical enquiry on finding the truth. He also relates happiness with liberty and individuality. Individual can discover his inner powers with the help of happiness and these powers can be developed through independent thought and expression. Liberty should not be enjoyed by the illiterate masses. He considers liberty as belonging to higher and advanced civilisations.

Thus, he supports negative liberty with absence of restraints. His liberty is applicable to mature individuals. He excludes children, invalids, the mentally handicapped and barbarian societies.

Mill's Views on Action = Ambedkarite Population

Mill divides all human action into two categories

1. Self-regarding actions
2. Other-regarding actions.

1. **Self-regarding Action = Raj-Rishi Ke Sabita**: Self-regarding actions are those actions in which the individual is allowed to do whatever he wants to do. He enjoys absolute freedom.
2. **Other-regarding Actions = Old Ambedkarite, New Dr Raj:** If individual actions affect other members of the society, these are known as other-regarding actions. State puts certain restrictions on the actions of the individual.

This division of individual actions is very confusing. It is very difficult to draw a line between self-regarding actions = Ambedkarji Ka View and other regarding actions of the individual = *Raj-Rishi Ke Sabita*. Moreover, individual action in one way or the other way affects the others.

He gives an example of a drunk-man or chain-smoker = Rasa Theory of Jammu School of Paintings. It is purely a self-regarding action as long as it does not affect the family and the society. The state neither interferes nor prohibits the sale of alcohol. But if it destroys the society, the state takes certain actions against it.

Number of political thinkers praised his views on liberty. Such as Professor Maxey states that Mill's chapter on freedom of thought and expression is one of the finest things in the political literature. Professor C. L. Wayper comments on ***The Essay on Liberty*** that no finer defence of liberty of thought and discussion has even been written.

Criticism = New View Point

1. J.S. Mill considers freedom of thought and expression as very essential for the development of the individual and the civilisation but he does not give the same freedom in the field of action.
2. Individual freedom promotes inequality among individuals.
3. Barker criticises Mill as "The Prophet of an empty liberty and an abstract individual." = Chamar History.
4. Macallum argues that Mill takes little account of the mysterious human thought like intuition, illumination and revelation.
5. Only, the literate, mature and individuals belonging to higher and advanced civilisation can enjoy the liberty.

Mill's Views on Women Equality = Dalit Samaj

J.S. Mill is the champion of individual liberty and value of the democratic institutions. At the same time, he also raised the voice for women equality not only inside the British Parliament but outside the Parliament also.

Prevailing Condition of Women in England

Social Status = Common Man Ke Approach: The social status of women in England was not good. They were neither free within marriage nor free to remain unmarried. They did not have freedom of choice. Women were the subordinate to men. Men expected obedience and affection from women. This was inculcated in the minds of women through education, training and socialisation. The society considered women as different from that of men. They were under suppression and domination of men. Moreover, he observed that men and women were under the influence of customs which restricted women in their social life.

Economic conditions = under developing country: J.S. Mill discussed the economic conditions of women in his important work "*Principles of Political Economy*" = *Ashoka Jaitely Ji Ke Story.* He argued that women received low wages because of two important reasons. Firstly, because of the traditional norms of the society and secondly, the female labour was easily available for unskilled job. In this way, both customs and law kept women away from seeking any means of livelihood other than mother and wife. Thus, they were deprived of jobs on par with men in public offices. They were thrown into the backgrounds on the basis of customs and prejudices = unlikes political view.

Political conditions = Check-Mate Rulers: The women and slaves had the similar conditions. They did not have the universal adult suffrage. Men enjoyed the absolute power. They were unable to take part in the political affairs of the state.

Mill fought for the rights and equality for women. He was very much influenced by his father James Mill, Bentham for his intellectual development, Harriet Taylor Mill, W.J. Fox, William Thompson and the Saint Simonians like Saint Bazard, Enfantin and Pierre Leroux etc. He made a strong claim for women's equality in his important work "***The Subjection of Women***" on the following three areas:

1. Women's right to vote
2. Right to equal opportunity in education
3. Employment.

His main consideration for women's equality was on woman as wife and mother. He ignored the picture of women as daughters, sisters or single women living alone or at the custody of parents.

His views on women's equality can be understood under the following headings:

1. Social Equality = No Jat-Pat:

(a) He made it clear being a free rational human being, she should enjoy her rights.

(b) He demanded for them freedom and opportunity. They could manage very well domestic affairs as well as career.

(c) He raised the demand for equality of the sexes before the law because he knew that the marriage did not provide them dignity and equal status. They were in a worse situation that they could not claim their children after leaving their husbands.

(d) He also supported a married Women's Property Bill in the British parliament.

(e) He emphasised on women Education.

(f) He believed in mutual respect and love and due regard to one another's rights after marriage.

(g) He defended the right of exceptional women to have their freedom of choice and to make the home a dignified and honourable place for those who preferred domestic work.

2. Economic Equality = Check on black-market + Zain-ul-Aibidin Ke Story:

(a) He was of the opinion that economic equality could be achieved only through education.

(b) He emphasised on women's property rights and earnings.

(c) He defended the women to choose a life other than motherhood and marriage.

(d) He also encouraged them to become business partners, philosophers, politicians and scientists.

(e) He related equal opportunity in education with opportunity in employment for women.

(f) He was in the favour of opening of the industry occupations freely to both men and women.

3. Political Equality = No Caste Bar:

1. Mill was very much confident about women's potential in politics and managing political affairs as compare to men. He quoted the examples of Joan of Arc, Elizabeth and Margaret of Austria. He made it clear in his another important work ***The Representative Government.***
2. He advocated the right of vote to women. Ultimately he succeeded in providing women the universal adult franchise i.e. right to vote.

Mill's Views on Representative Government = Capability

Mill discussed the types of government in his important work "***Representative Government***". He gave importance to representative democracy. It was very essential for the progress and development of the citizens. It proved useful in promoting virtue, intelligence and excellence. It also promoted the education among the citizens. It encouraged the freedom of thought and expression. A healthy atmosphere could be developed among the citizens. There would be possibility of the emergence of the wisest leaders in the state.

Dangers of Democracy = Brahmin Samaj

1. **Majority Rule as Dangerous = Dalit Status**: Mill was of the opinion that government run by the majority could be dangerous and tyrannical for the minorities of the state.
2. **Collective Mediocrity**: Collective mediocrity was not good for the successful functioning of the democracy because it

consisted of generally innocent, incapable and inefficient and less educated members of the controlling body or executive and legislature.

3. **Decentralisation of Power**: Decentralisation of power in democracy was another important danger because the powers were distributed among different sets like the parliament, cabinet, ministers, bureaucrats etc. so it was difficult to take quick decision for the welfare of the citizens.
4. **Relationship between Equality and Democracy**: He rejected the meaning of the equality in democracy as everyone to count for one and nobody to count for more than one. It was a false democracy. For him, the true democracy meant that intelligent persons should be given more weightage than the less intelligent persons. That could be the right type of relation between them.
5. **Misuse of Power = Brahmin Samaj:** He was very much afraid of the misuse of power by the selected few for their selfish interest = Indra Gandhi life history.

Thus, in order to avoid all these dangers of democracy, he developed the concept of representative government in democracy. The following are the some important characteristics of his representative government:

1. **Proportional Representation:** He believed in proportional representation. It gave plural votes to capable persons.
2. **Open Ballot = Brahminism:** He recommended open ballot instead of secret ballot. He was of the opinion that the voting was a public trust which "should be performed under the eye and criticism of the public."
3. **Plural Voting = Muslim Cantonment Area + Kashmir Issue:** He was the strong support of plural voting. For it, he prescribed for the checking of the performance and universal education for all children. Thus, he fixed education as an essential criterion for plural voting.

4. **Disqualification of the Citizen = High Moral Character:** He recommended the following disqualification of the citizen:
   (a) Those unable to pay local taxes;
   (b) Those dependent on public welfare;
   (c) Legal bankrupt and moral deviants like habitual drunkards.
5. **Right to Vote for Tax Payers:** He gave right to vote for those people who paid some prescribed minimum amount of taxes because he felt that tax would make both voters and legislators more responsible.
6. **Right to Vote for Women:** He favoured women for their political rights.
7. **Education:** He emphasised on the right type of education which made the citizens aware of their rights and duties.
8. **Unpaid Member of Parliament**: He was in the favour of paying of salaries to M.Ps. They should be treated as true representatives of the people and served the nation.
9. **Election Expenditure by the State**: He strongly recommended that candidates would not bear the expenditure on the election but state had to bear it.
10. **Bicameral Legislature**: He advocated the bicameral legislature. He gave importance to the second chamber for national interests. The true function of a parliament was not only to administer but to watch and supervise the administration also.

In short, his representative government aims at providing liberty of thought and expression, equality through education developing a sense of responsibility responsible citizens etc. His representative government was practicable in homogeneous group of citizens in a less populated state.

Relevance of Mill's Ideas on Modern State and Government

J.S. Mill has given a balanced political thought. At the one hand, he tried his best to provide individual liberty focusing on freedom of thought and expression and women equality by providing them right to vote. On the other hand, he gave the idea of representative government which was based on proportional representation and plural voting. No doubt, his main idea behind was the spread of education through which the people become literate, intellectual and responsible citizens. They might develop the sense of responsibility and duty towards the state.

This, his state was the product of the will of the people. His idea about the state was the result of active participation of the people.

His ideas on state and government are very relevant and useful. Most of the democratic states of the world are based on his ideas with certain modifications, e.g. the proportional representations in the representative government. Representative government is an indirectly democracy which is suitable for highly densed populated countries and run by the representatives of the people.

Secondly, the proportional representation is also applicable with certain modification. He advocated the system of proportional representation to ensure that all sections of the society got representation in proportion to its voting strength. Now, in modern period especially in India, where some sections of the society are in minority like SC/STs, there is provision of reservation of seats as territorial representation = superior Samaj.

He emphasised on the plural voting on the basis of voter's educational qualification tax-payers and property holders. Now, Education plays important role not only in politics but all others fields also. He was the strong supporter of true democracy which was run by intelligent rulers for the common good. To cite an example of America. He advocated a liberal state in a free society with positive role.

There are certain views of different political philosophers about the contributions of Mill to political science such as Maxey remarks that Mill's contribution on such important matters like election methods, second chamber, executive organisation, local government, federal government and the government of dependencies could not afford to ignore.

John Bowel ranked him high as logician, economist and political philosopher. He regarded him as a prophet in his own age. Professor C.L. Wayper says, "With the passage of time, On Liberty has grown in stature and meaning because its predictions have come to life more realistically and more tragically than seen possible in the middle of the nineteenth century when belief in the progress of liberty was well high universe."

He was the last utilitarian who made it more sensible and acceptable and practicable to the world. He gave a new direction to the world. His contribution and its relevance to political thought like emancipation of women and their suffrage, proportional representation, liberty, individualism, his realisation of the possibility of tyranny of majority rule, education etc. will always be remembered by the world= the philosophy of a Dalit-King historian + student of History = new discovery + Globle Warming Ka View = Computer Age Ke history = Socialism Ka Aagaz + transfer of power from Brahminism to Dalit Samaj = Englishtan Ke Identity found in the J and K State + mini Ladakh Ka View = Tiny Japan.

PART - II

Comparative Politics = Dalit History

Chapter - 6

Comparative Politics and Dalit History

Comparative politics is the most significant contribution to modern history of the political science. It has opened a new chapter of progress development and modernisation while comparing and competing among nations = Dalit vision. It is not only concerned with the comparison with the different governments of the world but also comparison in different fields like economic, social, cultural, games, sports, science and technology, public and private enterprises etc. The advent of means of transport and communication has given birth to Comparative Politics = Dalit Concept + good human soul = Dr Shabnam Grewal Ka Ghar.

It is based on analytical, empirical and scientific investigations of both developed and developing states. It helps the developing nations to understand the developed nations. At the same time, it provides these nations the ways for their further development.

Growth of Comparative Politics after 1947 from Narendra Modi to Raj-Rishi

The study of comparative politics became highly significant in 1950's with the efforts of American political scientists. But the existence of comparative politics can be traced in the writings of Aristotle who analysed the working of 158 Greek constitutions and classified the governments. He also gave the causes of revolutions and remedies of revolution. The growth of comparative politics can be understood through the following stages:

First Stage

Aristotle is also the father of Comparative Politics = Criminal + Faqir = New horizontal knowledge. His writings are the product of comparison in which he has tried his best to explain the organisation, nature, functions and qualities of an ideal state and the best practicable state. He applied comparative method for investigation of the different types of state. Other political thinkers like Polybius, Cicero, Machievalli, De Tocqueville, Bryce, Ostrogorski, Max Weber, J.S. Mill, and Jean Bodin etc. used the comparative method of study. Comparative method aims at the study of present politics from the past history, e.g. the Writings of the Roman thinkers like Polybius and Cicero carried the Greek ideas to Roman thought. Machievalli's important works The Prince and The discourses also involved ideas from Roman history.

Second Stage

The contributions of some political thinkers like Samuel H. Beer, M. Hass, and Bernard Ulam etc. can be kept in the second stage. During this stage, the emphasis was given on instrument of institutional comparisons, political system = local-self government of Lord Ripon.

Third Stage

Third stage includes the important contributions of David Easton, Gabriel A. Almond, James C. Coleman, Karl Deutsch, Powell, Harold Lasswell, Robert A. Dahl, Edward Shills, Harry Eckstein, David Apter, Lucian Pye, Sidney Verba, Myron Weiner etc. These writers have used their own vocabulary in comparative politics e.g. Easton given his system approach using the words like inputs, outputs, demands, supports feedback. Karl Deutsch borrows a cybernetic language which applies to political systems the concept of feedback of various types—autonomy, memory, load, lag, lead and gain, receptors, communication etc. = Vaishya Community of Kashmir.

The term '*politics*' in the field of comparative politics consists of the following three connotations-

1. Political activity

2. Political process
3. Political power.

1. **Political Activity:** Political activity simply means actions taken by the different political institutions in the forms of the decisions, policies or plans. Moreover, it provides resolutions to any kind of conflict for the interests of the people. Thus, it aims at reduction of the tension and resolution of conflicts. In other words, arising conflicts, demands for their solution and the efforts in this regards constitute political activity.
2. **Political Process:** Second important connotation of comparative politics is the political process. It is the extension of the political activity. It includes governmental and non-governmental agencies. Here, non-governmental agencies play important role. These agencies influence the government of the state for protecting and promoting their specific interests. It is the process of interaction between the groups, associations and government. It allows the private associations existing in the state to influence the government and participate in the policy formulation of the government.
3. **Political Power:** The study of politics revolves round the power. The meaning of comparative politics also includes the subject of political power. Friedrich has defined the term power as "a certain kind of human relationship." Tawney defines it as "the capacity of an individual, or a group of individuals or groups in the manner in which he desires". Lasswell and Kaplan define political power as, "the capacity of affecting the behaviour of another person by the threat of some form of sanction." Alan Ball is of the opinion, "Greater the sanction, or the more numerous the sanction, the greater will be the political power." Thus, political power stands for a type of permission or sanction. The political power in comparative politics includes the study of the state and government on one hand and on the other hand, it is the study of the exercise of power in the form of sanctions, its role in decision-making matters etc.

Definitions

1. According to M.G. Smith, “Comparative Politics is the study of the forms of political organisations, their properties, correlations, variations and modes of change.”
2. In the words of Ronald H. Chilcote, “comparative Politics studies a broad range of political activity, including governments and their institutions as well as other forms of Organisations not directly related to national government; for example, tribes, communities, associations, unions etc.”
3. According to M. Curtis, “Comparative Politics is concerned with significant regularities, similarities and differences in the working of political institutions and political behaviour.”
4. In the words of Lasswell and Kaplon, “Comparative Politics is also concerned with the norms, basic beliefs and values underlying political activity.”
5. Howard J. Wiarda defines, “The field of comparative politics involves the systematic and comparative study of nations and their political systems.”
6. According to Briabante, “Comparative Politics is the identification and the interpretation of factors in the whole social order which appear to affect whatever political functions and their institutions which have been identified and listed for comparison.”
7. In the words of E.A. Freeman, “Comparative politics is comparative analysis of the various forms of government and diverse political institutions.”
8. According to Almond Powell, Strom and Dalton, “Comparative Politics is the study of political systems, not as isolated cases but through generalisations and comparisons.”
9. In the words of Braibante, “Comparative politics is the identification and the interpretation of factors in the whole social order which appear to affect whatever political functions and their institutions which have been identified and listed for comparison.”

On the basis of above written definitions, it can be concluded that the meaning of comparative politics consists of political activity, political process and political power.

Distinction between Comparative Government and Comparative Politics in Art Form = Mughalian styled Culture. (1526 - 1707).

The terms comparative government and comparative politics are closely related to each other. These terms are used interchangeably. Writers like Alan Ball, Freeman and Jean Blondel etc. have established a link between the comparative government and comparative politics. On the other hand some political thinkers like Michael Curtis, Ronald Chilcote etc. have differentiated between the two.

Definitions of Comparative Government

1. According to Jean Blondel, "Comparative government involves a study of the pattern of national governments in the contemporary world."
2. In the opinion of G.K. Roberts, "Comparative Government is the study of states and the governmental institutions and processes on a comparative basis."
3. In the words of Freeman, "By comparative government, I mean comparative study of political institutions and forms of government."
4. Edward Freeman writes, "It is comparative analysis of the various forms of government and diverse political institutions."

Comparative Government	*Comparative Politics*
1. Comparative government is a narrow term. 2. It covers a comparative study of different systems, their institutions and functions. 3. It covers the comparative study of the European countries only.	1. It is a broader term. 2. It includes the non-governmental institutions and non-state political contexts like political socialisation, political conflict resolutions, bargaining, communication, decision-making, political culture, political development etc.

(Contd...)

4. It is concerned with behaviour, institutions, processes ideas and values of one nation.
5. It is based on the study of executive, legislature, judiciary, political parties and pressure groups and constitutions of the European nations.
6. It is not concerned with significant regularities, similarities and differences in the working of political institutions and political behaviour.
7. It is an old concept which ignores the dynamic factors that accounts for change in politics.
8. It is descriptive in approach so it is limited in nature and scope.
9. The comparative study in comparative government is based on one standard system of politics. In other words, it has monographic basis.
10. It is only a theoretical work.
11. The chief exponents of comparative government are John Marriott, Arthur Keith, James Bryce, Ivor Jennings, Dicey, Robson, Woodrow Wilson etc.
12. It helps in building a theory of ideal political institutions.

3. It includes the comparatives study of both European countries as well as new nations of Asia, Africa and Latin America.
4. It is concerned with behaviour, institutions processes, ideas and values of different nations.
5. It is based on the study of a broader range of political activities including formal and informal organs of the governments even tribes, communities, and groups etc. of non-European nations.
6. It is concerned with significant regularities, similarities and differences in the working of political institutions and political behaviour.
7. It is new concept which is based on empirical studies - hypothesis, data, observation, experiments, verification, scientific methods etc.
8. It is scientific and empirical in nature and scope so it covers a wide range of other fields also like economics, sociology, psychology anthropology, environmental sciences etc.
9. The comparative study in comparative politics is multi-dimensional. It covers the study of political culture, political socialisation, political development, political participation, political elites, political systems, etc. of European nations.
10. It is concerned with politics-power relationship.
11. The chief exponents of comparative politics are Almond, Powel, Verba, David Easton, David Apter, Robert A. Dahl etc.
12. It helps to build a scientific theory of politics. It also aims at further new researches - macro to micro.

Nature of Comparative Politics

1. **Empirical, Scientific and Analytical Study of Politics:** The nature of comparative politics is based on empirical, scientific and analytical study of politics. It involves the activities of the governments and their structures and functions.
2. **Emphasis on Value-Free Theory:** Comparative politics rejects the traditional approaches and emphasis on the scientific approach which give value-free theory.
3. **Emphasis on the Study of Infrastructure of Politics:** Comparative politics focuses on the study of infrastructures of politics such as political systems, sub-systems, individual behaviour, role of race, religion, elites, political parties, pressure and interest groups, associations etc.
4. **Inter-Disciplinary Approach**: The nature of comparative politics is focused on inter-disciplinary approach. It means that its study takes into considerations other disciplines also like psychology, sociology, economics, and anthropology and even from natural sciences like biology.
5. **Equal Importance to Both Developed and Developing Countries:** Comparative politics gives importance to the study of political processes and systems of both developed and developing nations, European and non-European nations. Modern political writers like Almond, Powell, Verba, David Easton, Edward Shills, and Coleman etc. have given importance to the study of politics of the developing nations-Asian, African and Latin American countries.
6. **Both Horizontal and Vertical Comparative Studies:** Comparative politics consists of both horizontal and vertical comparative studies. Horizontal study means a comparative study of the political structures and functions, processes and institutions etc. of different countries. On the other hand, vertical studies stand for a comparative study of the political structures and sub-systems at work within a country.
7. **Scientific Theory-Building Approach:** Comparative politics builds a scientific theory after making comparative

studies of the similarities and dissimilarities of different political systems.

8. **Research Methodology:** The research conducted in comparative politics is based on scientific methods like interview, questionnaire, random sampling, data collection, observation etc.
9. **Development of New Concepts:** It has developed many new concepts in the study of comparative politics like political, culture, political development and modernisation, political systems, political socialisation, political sociology, political simulation, political elite, political environment etc.

Scope of Comparative Politics = Presidential Democracy

The scope of comparative politics is very broader which includes the study of all political activities, political processes and political powers of different countries. It consists of comparative study of the regularities, similarities and differences among the structures and functions of different political systems of the world. The following are some important points for the scope of Comparative Politics:

1. **Study of Political Structures:** The scope of comparative politics includes the study of political structures of formal and informal institutions of government including legislature, executive, judiciary, bureaucracy, pressure and interest groups, political parties and their types etc.
2. **Study of Political Functions:** It deals with the study of political functions like interest articulation, interest aggregation, political communication, rule-making, rule-application, decision-making etc. of different political systems.
3. **Study of Political Behaviour:** Comparative politics deal with the study of political behaviour of the people in the process of politics. Political behaviour consists of political participation voting behaviour, leadership, recruitment, mass politics, political elite, populism political socialisation etc.
4. **Study of Modern Approach:** It deals with the study of modern approaches which are based on fact-laden study of

politics such as behavioural approach, Marxian approach, sociological, psychological, economic system approaches etc.

5. **Comparative Study of Political Institutions and Structures:** It is the study of political institutions and structures of different countries. These institutions consist of party politics, party system, pressure group politics, types of states etc.

6. **Study of Power, Influence, Authority and Legitimacy:** Comparative politics also deals with the study of the concepts of power, influence authority and legitimacy along with their differences and relationships.

7. **Study of Political Culture:** Political culture is the collective disposition of political belief, political attitude, political behaviour values etc. of a society. These political beliefs and values have certain affect on the working of each political system. Thus, the study of political culture plays a significant role in the scope of comparative politics.

8. **Study of Political Socialisation**: Political socialisation is a process through which the political cultures are maintained and transferred from one generation to another. Thus, the study of political socialisation is also included in the scope of comparative politics.

9. **Study of Political Development:** Political development is identified with social, administrative, economic and cultural developments. It also deals with the study of political development.

10. **Study of Political Participation and Voting Behaviour:** It includes the study of political participation and voting behaviour of the people. It gives a good account of comparative study of political participation and voting behaviour in different types of governments like in democratic or dictatorial form of government.

11. **Study of Political Elites:** It also includes the study of political elites. Every society is ruled by a group of minority

those who possess the qualities necessary to rule or to exercise full social and political powers.

12. **Study of Political Ideologies:** It also takes into consideration the study of political ideologies like Nazism, Fascism, Marxism, Socialism etc.
13. **Study of Types of Government:** It deals with the study of different types of governments like democracy, authoritarian regime, unitary and federal forms, parliamentary and presidential forms of government etc.
14. **Study of New Global Concepts:** It deals with the study of new global concepts like globalisation, environmental issues, human rights, women empowerment and emancipation etc.

Chapter - 7

Modern Approaches to the Study of Comparative Politics=Sudra State of Mind

Approach is a technique to find a solution to any problem occurring in a given society. In social sciences, especially in the field of political science, approaches are also applied for theory-building = Kashmir remains. Approach is a wider term which helps a researcher to identify the problem i.e. what the problem is? And how to solve it? For the selection and solution of the problem, the researcher uses various methods (deductive or inductive or scientific). On the basis of various methods, the approaches are divided into two categories:

1. Traditional/Normative Approaches = Old Quran + Idiot MP. Karra.
2. Modern Approaches = Dalit Samaj.

Traditional Approaches = Anti-Dalit Propaganda

Traditional approaches are also known as normative or classical approaches. These approaches deal the politics with the study of state and government and its various organs. These approaches to comparative politics were in practice till the World War. The scholars of these approaches put emphasis on descriptive, historical and legalistic subjects. The study of the 'foreign governments' believed on the written documents. Moreover, these approaches focused on the Western European democracies. These approaches are of four types.

(i) Philosophical approach = Dalit King Ashok and his race.
(ii) Historical approach = Nam-Theory.
(iii) Legal approach = Social-History of the Dalit Samaj.
(iv) Institutional approach = Barnai Dal Ke Dastana.

Importance Characteristics of Traditional Approaches

1. These are based on the study of formal institutions and neglect the political processes.
2. These are focused on the Western European political system and neglected the non-Western European political systems.
3. These emphasis on the description of existing institutions with little attention given to the analysis and the development of systematic generalisations about the political phenomena.
4. These are non-comparative approaches.
5. These are parochial in nature.
6. They give no place to any other social sciences.
7. There is lack of concern for the development of theories through scientific investigations like collection of data, measurement, verification, sampling etc. in order to test the specific hypotheses.
8. These are cultural bound.
9. These lack methodology.

Dalit Approache

Dalit approache to the study of comparative politics are the reaction against the traditional approaches. Modern approaches are based on the study of political system, political processes and patterns of political behaviour of the people. They give importance to scientific methods for conducting comparative politics researches. They emphasis on fact-laden study of politics. There are number of modern approaches to the study of comparative politics like behavioural approach, Marxian approach, quantitative approach, psychological approach, sociological approach, economic approach, systems approach, structural-functional approach, etc. = Dalit Samaj Ki History.

Systems and Structural-Functional Approach

The origin of the systems = Dr B.S. Nand Ke Kitab + his scientific approach can be found in the general systems theory. The origin of the general systems is impressed by the writings of a biologist Ludwig Von Bertallanfy in 1920s. Meanwhile, after the World War II = a complete history of J and K State; a number of scholars from different disciplines began to write about the unification of sciences with social sciences. They were of the opinion that there were a number of common things in each discipline. Hence, with their efforts, the System Theory became popular in the mid-fifties. David Easton, G.A. Almond Powell, Morton Kaplan etc. were the important contributors in this system theory in the field of political science.

Meaning and Definitions of System

1. **Ludwig Von Bertalanffy** describes system as "a set of elements standing in interaction."
2. **Hall and Fagen** define system as "a set of objects together with relations between the objects and between their attitudes."
3. In the words of **Collin Cherry,** "A system is a whole which is compounded of many parts- an ensemble of attitudes."
4. According to **Concise Oxford Dictionary,** "It is (1) Complex whole, set of connected things or parts, organised body of material or immaterial things; (2) Method, organisation, considered principles of procedure a physical system is one whose components are concrete entities, an analytical system is an intellectual construction composed of aspects or attributes of concrete entities."
5. In the opinion of **Morton A. Kaplan,** "A brief and non-technical description of the object of systems analysis would include: the study of a set of interrelated variables, as distinguished from the environment of the set, and of the ways in which this set is maintained under the impact of environmental disturbances."
6. According to **Almond,** "A system means attributing a particular set of properties to interactions in a society."

Structural-Functional Approach by Gabriel A. Almond and Powell

Structural-functional approach is not a new approach to the study of comparative politics. Its origin may be traced back in the writings of Plato and Aristotle. Structural-functional approach was first adopted in different disciplines of social sciences like Anthropology and Sociology. Radcliffe-Brown and B. Malinowski applied this approach in their investigations in the field of Anthropology. On the other hand, Merton and Talcott Parsons used this approach in Sociology. In Political Science, the structural-functional approach was first applied in 1960 by Gabriel Almond and James S. Coleman to the study of non-Western politics.

Almond and Powell have given the structural-functional approach to the study of comparative politics. They have studied the political systems of the western countries firstly especially the U.S.A. and U.K. Then, they concentrated on the non-Western countries. They have recognised a midpoint in the process of development which they called 'transitional'. Hence, the political development is regarded as a change from a traditional system through transitional stage to the modern system. The Western political system is regarded as the model; and all traditional societies are running towards it.

Almond defines a political system as "that systems of interactions to be found in all independent societies which perform the function of integration and adaption by means of the employment, or threat of employment, of more or less legitimate physical compulsion."

I. Common Properties: Almond is of the opinion that political systems are different from each other but they have following four common properties-

1. All political systems have their own political structures.
2. All political systems have certain common political functions.
3. Political structures perform a number of functions.
4. All political systems have the mixed character of both cultures i.e. modern and traditional elements.

II. Characteristics: According to him, political system has the following three important characteristics:

1. Comprehensiveness
2. Interdependence
3. Boundaries.

1. **Comprehensiveness:** For Almond, comprehensiveness means interactions of both input and output in a political system. It includes not only the structures created by law like legislature, law courts, bureaucracy etc. but also political parties, interest and pressure groups, the mass-media etc.
2. **Inter-dependence:** It means that a change in one sector of interactions brings changes in other sectors also. To quote the changes in the technology of communications have brought changes in the electoral process, the characteristics of political parties, the legislature and the executive. The concepts of system and interdependence lead us to look for these changes when any specific role changes significantly.
3. **Boundaries:** Third important characteristic of political system is the existence of boundaries. It means that "there are points where other systems end and the political system begins."

III. Classification of Functions: Almond has given seven-fold classification of functions performed by a political system under two headings:

1. Input Functions
2. Output Functions.

1. **Input Functions (Political Functions):** According to him, the input functions are performed by non-government sub-system, by the society and the general environment. These functions are political in nature. For him, the input functions are more important in the political systems of the developing countries. These are four in number:—
   (i) Political Socialisation and Recruitment
   (ii) Interest Articulation

(iii) Interest Aggregation

(iv) Political Communication.

(i) Political Socialisation and Recruitment: According to Almond and Verba, "Political socialisation is the process by which political cultures are maintained and changed." It is also very helpful to transform the political cultures from one generation to another. It is a psychological concept in nature.

In the words of Almond, "All political systems tend to perpetuate their culture and structures through which the young pass, though the process continues through adult life. These structures include the family, the church, the school, the work group, voluntary associations, and media of communication, political parties and government institutions."

Political recruitment begins where the general political socialisation ends. It means the recruitment of citizens into the specialised role of the political system. It gives birth to political leaders. Again the political recruitment process involves the members of the society out of various sub-cultures such as religious communities, castes, classes, ethnic communities etc. It differs from country to country, for example, the Western societies believe in achieved values whereas the Asian societies give weightage to the ascribed values like kinship, caste, religion etc.

(ii) Interest Articulation: For him, "Interest articulation is concerned with the formulation and expression, claims and demands for political action." It is the voice for political demands of the people to the decision-makers. In other words, it is the process by which the individuals or groups make demands upon the political decision-makers. It is the first functional step in the political conversion process.

He has given the following four main interest articulation structures:

(a) Institutional interest groups include legislatures, political executives, bureaucracies, armies, churches etc.

(b) **Non-associational interest groups** includes kinship lineage, ethnic, regional, religious, status and class groups.

(c) **Anomic interest groups** are concerned with spontaneous breakthrough into the political system from the society such as riots, demonstrations etc. = Kashmir Issue + Dr Burhan Wani Ke Kisay.

(d) **Associational interest groups** consist of specialised structures such as trade unions, businessmen or industrialists, ethnic associations, associations organised by educational associations etc.

(iii) Interest Aggregation: The management of political demands by the political parties, interest groups etc. is known as interest aggregation. For him, "Interest aggregation is achieved either by the formulation of general policies in which interests which have been articulated may be combined, accommodated and compromised or by the recruitment of political personnel who are more or less committed to a particular pattern of policy." He gives importance to party system for aggregative functions. Thus, he classifies party system into four systems:

(a) Authoritarian systems
(b) Dominant non-authoritarian system
(c) Competitive two-party system
(d) Competitive multi-party systems.

He, further, gives the following three categories of political parties on the basis of their aggregative functions:

(a) Secular, pragmatic, bargaining parties
(b) Absolute, value-oriented or ideological parties
(c) Particularistic or traditional parties.

(iv) Political Communication: Political communication is a bridge between the masses and the political administration. All functions of political socialisation and recruitment, interest articulation, interest aggregation, even the output functions are performed by the means of communication. It makes the people remain in touch with

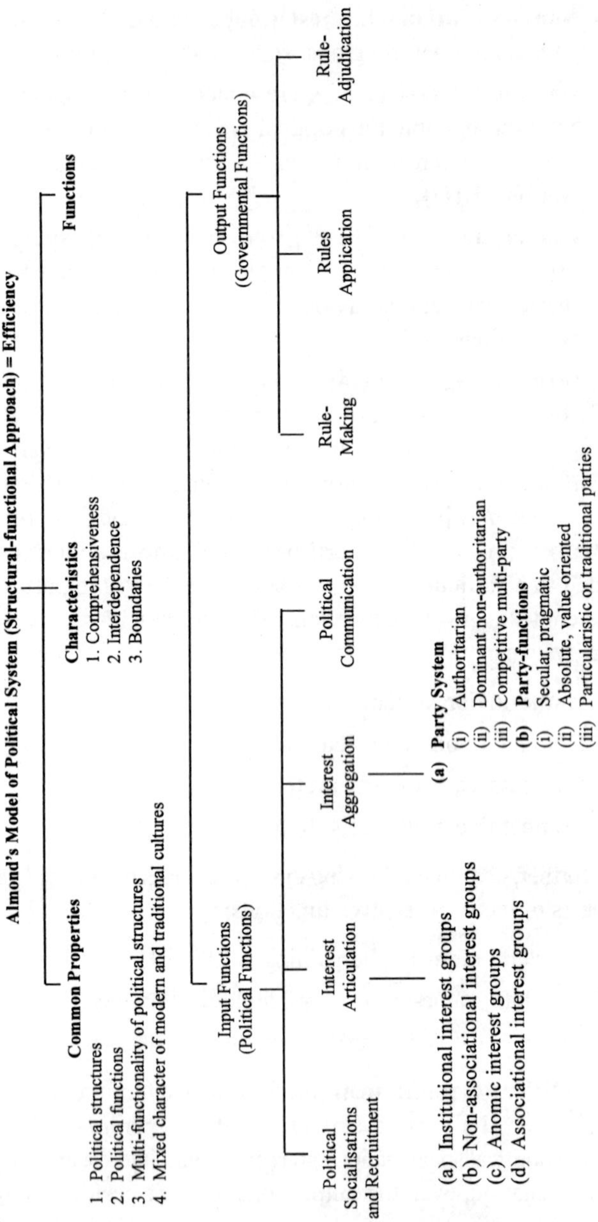
Almond's Model of Political System (Structural-functional Approach) = Efficiency
Common Properties
1. Political structures
2. Political functions
3. Multi-functionality of political structures
4. Mixed character of modern and traditional cultures
Characteristics
1. Comprehensiveness
2. Interdependence
3. Boundaries
Functions
Input Functions (Political Functions)
Output Functions (Governmental Functions)
Political Socialisations and Recruitment
Interest Articulation
Interest Aggregation
Political Communication
Rule-Making
Rules Application
Rule-Adjudication
(a) Institutional interest groups
(b) Non-associational interest groups
(c) Anomic interest groups
(d) Associational interest groups
(a) Party System
(i) Authoritarian
(ii) Dominant non-authoritarian
(iii) Competitive multi-party
(b) Party-functions
(i) Secular, pragmatic
(ii) Absolute, value oriented
(iii) Particularistic or traditional parties

the political system. He identifies it with blood circulation. For him, "Political communication is the crucial boundary maintenance function. Autonomy of the media makes for a free flow of information from the society to the polity and from one political structure to another, as well as an open feed-back from output to input again."

2. Out-put Functions (Governmental Functions): He has given the following three output functions of a political system:

(i) Rule-Making

(ii) Rule-Application

(iii) Rule-Adjudication.

(i) **Rule-Making:** Rule-making is the traditional legislative function. For him, rule-making consists of either charismatic process or slow process in the primitive societies. Rule-making processes exist in different forms in all political systems. In simple political systems, the rule-making process lies in the hands of groups of adult males whereas in the monarchy, it involves the kings or Council of Officials. In contemporary developed political systems, it is performed by the parliaments.

(ii) **Rule-Application**: Rule application traditionally means executive organ of the government. Its main task is to enforce the rules and policies made by the rule-making authority in one form or the other. In modern times, the rules are executed by officials who need a very high degree of administrative capacity. Thus, there is close link between the executive and the bureaucracy.

(iii) **Rule-Adjudication**: Traditionally it means judiciary which interprets the laws, rules and regulation. Moreover, it means that rules should not be violated. If these are violated, the penalties must be specified and imposed. It also aims at resolving the conflicts. Almond defines, it as "The performance of the adjudication function involves the process of making authoritative decisions as to whether or not a rule has been transgressed in a given case."

Criticism = New Discovery

1. Almond has not defined the meaning of the system and independent societies.

2. His analysis is not applicable to the non-Western societies.
3. His list of seven-fold function is full of shortcomings because he has not drawn a boundary between political and non-political functions.
4. He has not given enough importance to the output functions.
5. He has failed to give importance to the feedback process.
6. He has recognised the importance of political communication as input function but has failed to recognise its importance at output and feedback levels.
7. His approach has ignored the study of crisis and revolution.
8. His approach has excluded the study of role of individuals.
9. His approach gives less importance to the study of the structures.
10. His approach gives no place to the study of values and goals.

Political Economy and Dependency Approach (A.G. Frank)

Since the time immemorial, the economy plays a very important role in the state. The monarchy system was based on the generation of economy while levying taxes, octroi etc. on the general masses that was one of the forms of political economy in the ancient era. Thus, in other words, when economy is influenced by the politics, it is called as political economy.

Meaning and Definitions of Political Economy = Good Human Soul

The word 'Economics' has been derived from the Greek two words 'Oikos' and 'Nomos' - former means 'home' and later means 'law' or 'order'. Thus, it means to signify the management or arrangement of the material part of household or domestic affairs. It aims at avoiding of waste.

The term political economy is used for studying production and trade and their relations with law, custom and government as well as with the distribution of national income and wealth. It has moral philosophical origin. It was developed in the eighteenth century as the study of economies of states.

The term political economy was first used by Antoine de Montchretien in his important work "*Treatise on Political Economy*". Adam Smith, David Ricardo, Henry George and Karl Marx etc. are the some of the chief exponents of political economy = Omar censures Mehbooba for *'unprecedented clampdown'* on Id = Ego problem among Muslims.

Adam Smith, the father of economics, gave a powerful impulse to the study of political economy also. His important and great work "An Inquiry into the Nature and Cause of the Wealth of Nations" is based on political economy.

Political economy is related to the system in which economic structure is studied within the established political structure. It is related to the decision of economic matters. The view regarding the economic functioning of the state has been changed from classical to modern thinkers. They were interested in studying whether to allow private forces to work independently or the state interference is must to achieve the welfare objectives.

The classical thinkers were in the favour of doctrine of laissez-faire i.e. non-interference of the state in the economic matters of the society. They believed in complete economic liberty. All the economic decisions must be dictated by the market forces. They considered state as a necessary evil which could not do any good thing but plenty of bad things. Thus, state kept its hand off in the economic matters and allowed the market forces to operate independently and freely. The function of the state was only to maintain law and order in the society.

Ricardo favoured the policy of non-interference. He regarded government services as unproductive because they did not produce wealth but still he justified government action in certain areas of national importance. Karl Marx assumed economic functions must be discharged not by state but by the producers (workers) themselves.

In modern time, the modern economists have taken state as a welfare state. Hence, there should be interference of the state in the economic matters of the society because sometimes situation goes out of the control of market forces where it becomes essential for state to interfere. Hence, they have approved the role of state in maintaining the economic and social justices in modern time. State has emerged as a welfare state.

Dependency Approach by A.G. Frank = Army deployed, Curfew continued in Rajouri and Bhaderwah towns after religious classes = Blind Faith Ka glimpse

Dependency is a comparative concept of analysing the third world countries in Asia, Africa and Latin America. The concept of dependency has been emerging as the most important and interesting debates in the field of comparative analysis of the third world countries. It evolved in Latin America during the 1960s and emerged as a critique to Political Development Theory.

Its origin can be traced in Latin America in 1950s and 1960s. Latin America was a great supplier of primary products which it exchanged for the manufactures of the industrial world. But still it was underdeveloped. Thus, UN's Economic Commission for Latin America (ECLA), under the Argentinean economist Raul Prebisch and UN conference on Trade and Development (UNCTAD) were established to find out backwardness and under development of Latin America and other Third World countries. These countries acted as vehicle of exploitation inspite of increasing development. It was observed that the world was divided into two-

(i) Developed Countries (the Centres) = Delhi State.

(ii) Underdeveloped countries (the Periphery) = U.P., H.P., M.P. etc.

This division of the world was responsible for the under-development of the underdeveloped countries (Latin America and other Third World Countries) = Mobile services + Internet with Guruji and social harmony. Thus, the dependency of the periphery was being exploited by the centre to its own advantages. In this way, the gap between the centre and periphery on economic-industrial-technological gap began increasing. Latin America became dependent upon the international system, which was being dominated by the developed countries. There are two major approaches to study the dependency theory:

(a) Reformist Approach = Dalit History.

(b) Marxist Approach = Labour Concept.

(a) Reformist Approach: Fernando Henrique, Cardoso, Enzo Faletto, Osvaldo Sunkel, Celso Furtado, Helio Jaguaribe, Aldo Ferror and Anibal Pinto are the chief exponents of reformist approach for the study of dependency theory. They are closely associated with ECLA (the UN sponsored Economic Commission for Latin America). Being structuralists and nationalists, they seek to increase the degree of national autonomy over the internal development process.

(b) Marxist Approach: Ruy Mauro Marini, Theotonio Dos Santos, Andre Gunder Frank, Oscar Braun, Vania Bambirra, Anibal Quijano, T.A. Vasconi, Alonso Aguilar and Antonio Garcia etc. are the main supporters of Marxists approach for the study of dependency theory.

Dependency Theory: Andre Gundes Frank

A.G. Frank contributed a lot in the development of the Dependency Theory. His analysis of dependency theory is found in his central idea of the development of underdevelopment. He selected Brazil and Chile for his study. He used the term metropole as centre for the Western World and 'satellite' as periphery for third world. For him, metropolis and satellite divided this world in which metropolis exploited satellites. He explained his theory based on 'surplus extraction' in his important work *"Capitalism and Underdevelopment in Latin America"* = *Kashmir Issue + Damara class.*

He explained the phenomenon of underdevelopment in terms of the development of capitalism in the Western countries. He was of the opinion that periphery remained underdeveloped because of development and expansion of the developed West. Hence, dependency is a conditioning situation which put limits on the development of periphery.

Underdevelopment is a historical product of the relation between Metropolis and Satellites. The world consists of some metropolitan economics which govern, hinder and distort the development of a large number of satellites.

He has given three important contradiction of capitalism which are responsible for the underdevelopment of satellites:

1. **Contradiction of Expropiration /Appropriation of the Economic Surplus = Black-Marketing View of Abdullaha Family:** monopoly structure. It has capitalist links among themselves. It has a chain linkage system. It extends the capitalist link between the capitalist world and the national metropolises to the regional centres and from these to the local centres etc. It shows the exploitive nature of the World Capitalist System.
2. **Metropolis-Satellite Polarisation:** For him, this polarisation means even if there are structural differences but still there is qualitative relation so far their economic development or underdevelopment is concerned. It further means that metropolis economic development leads towards satellite's underdevelopment.

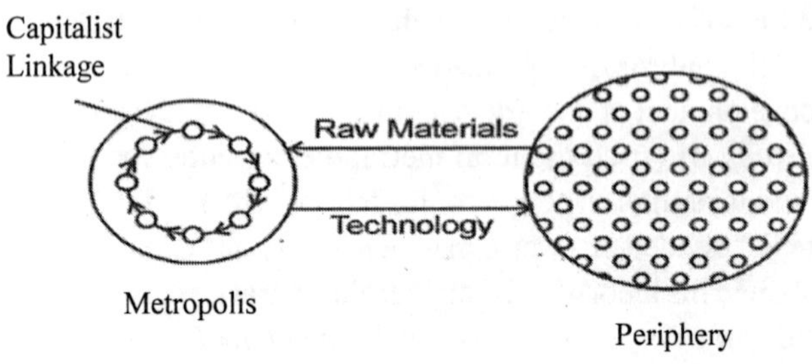

3. **Continuity in Change:** For him, continuity in change is responsible for the underdevelopment of the underdeveloped countries because the extention and development of the capitalist system has maintained its structure and contradictions intact. Thus, in the way, it has been a source of continued under-development of the under-developed countries.

Suggestions = Saudi Arabia + Mecca, Madina Ka Dora + Chamar History Ka Document

At the same time, he has given various suggestions to get rid of the chronic problems of underdevelopment of the underdeveloped countries:

1. **Bourgeoise Living as Real Enemy:** He believes in identifying the real enemy of underdevelopment. For him, bourgeoise living is the real enemy. It acts within every dependent country. It is an agent of neo-imperialism.
2. **Socialist Revolution = Chamar History:** He is in the favour of socialist revolution which may be able to overthrow of the existing structure of Metropolis-Satellite relations. With the help of socialist revolution, the underdevelopment can be removed. Raj-Rishi ka unpublished material = *Dalits and their Education' 'Dalit Literature and Kashmir History'* (600-1200); and 'Mohammad. Prophet and his Teaching' a new discourse.

Chapter - 8

Political Culture=To Chase the Damaras

Political culture plays a very significant role in the study of comparative politics. Political culture is a collected disposition of political beliefs, political attitudes, political values, political norms, political behaviour etc. of a given society. The term political culture was first used by Almond in 'Comparative Political System' published in 1956 as the story of Indian Constitional expert, Dr B.R. Ambedkar. Political Culture had been popularised by some of the leading American writers like Samuel Bear, Admulams and Gabriel A. Almond. It has become an important tool for the study of comparative politics = Dalit-history.

Definitions and Harwar's view: Work is Worship

1. According to A.R. Ball, "Political culture is composed of the attitudes, beliefs, emotions and values of society that relates to the political systems and to political issues."
2. In the words of Almond and Powell, "Political culture is the pattern of individual attitudes and orientations towards politics among the members of a political system."
3. Beer and Ulam state, "Certain aspects of the general culture of a society are especially concerned with how government ought to be conducted and what it shall try to do. This sector of culture we call political culture."
4. According to Lucian Pye, "Political culture is the set of attitudes, beliefs and sentiments that give order and meaning to a political process and that provides the underlying

assumptions and rules that govern behaviour in the political system".

5. In the opinion of R.C. Macridis, "Political culture is a commonly shared goals and commonly accepted rules."
6. In the words of Kavangh, "Political Culture is a short-hand expression to denote the emotional and attitudinal environment within which the political system operates."
7. Eric Rowe observes, "A Political Culture is a pattern of individual values, beliefs and emotional attitudes".
8. According to Pye and Sidney Verba, "Political culture consists of the system of empirical beliefs, expressive symbols and values which define the situation in which political action takes place."

The concept of political culture finds place in the subjective realm. According to Almond and Powell, it involves three components:

1. **Cognitive Orientations = fit body** implying knowledge, accurate or otherwise, of the political system.
2. **Affective Orientation = State forward Knowledge + Dr S.P. Gargotra Ka Rista** implying feelings of attachment, involvement, rejection, and like about political objects.
3. **Evaluative Orientations = Nam-history** implying judgments and opinions about the political objects + Kashmiri, Karnataka events.

Types of Political Culture = Sudra Concept

Almond and Verba have classified political culture into the following three types on the basis of distribution of general attitudes towards the political system and input-output processes:

- Parochial Political Culture
- Subject Political Culture
- Participant Political Culture.

1. **Parochial Political Culture:** People, who have little or no awareness of the political system, constitute parochial political culture. In other words, it includes those people

who are not interested in the input process and not aware of the output process. Majority of this kind of people are found in the traditional societies e.g. African societies. There is low cognitive of political objects. The people have no awareness of national political system. The society is traditional and backward.

2. **Subject Political Culture:** This type of political culture exists where there is high frequency of orientations towards a political system as a whole and towards specifically output aspects. It finds in dependent colonies where the people either feel pride or cultivate hostility towards their political system. They have only two choices— either to accept the governmental decisions of their rulers as legitimate or start struggle against them in the name of their right to self-determination, e.g. Asian societies.
3. **Participant Political Culture = Truth Prevailing History:** In this type of political culture, people are aware of the structures and the process of political system. They actively participate in all inputs and output structures. They make demands on the political system. For this, they form political parties, pressure groups, interest groups lobbies, associations etc. This type of political culture is found in a highly developed societies where people participate actively in the political activities. They are also conscious of their rights and duties, e.g. Western societies + Kashmir Issue.

Mixed Political Culture = Inferior to Superior

Again, Almond is of the opinion that no political culture exists in its pure form. It has mixed characteristics. Thus, he further has given the following four mixed type of political culture:

1. The Parochial-Subject Political Culture
2. The Subject-Participant Political Culture
3. The Parochial-Participant Political Culture.

The Civic Culture = Amit Shah Ke Soch

Civic culture is a participant political culture in which the political culture and political structure are congruent, e.g. the American society has civic culture because the Americans are very much involved in politics and also have a high civic competence.

Other Political Cultures = Leh Kumbh + Kargil Shiaities Muslims

1. Mass Culture: Every society consists of two types of political culture on the basis of power i.e. Elite Political Culture and Mass Political culture.

(a) **Elite Political Culture = Ginni Mahi of Punjab:** Those people who deal with power and have responsibilities for taking decisions of the government falls in this category. It is reflected in national planners, leaders, bureaucrats and among the English speaking intelligentsia in India.

(b) **Mass Political Culture = Dalit Samaj of Jalandhar:** Those people who simply observe the political system or participate in marginal activities, form mass political culture.

Determinants of Political Culture = New Discovery

A political culture is based on the attitudes, beliefs, faith, values and behaviour of the people towards their political system. It is the product of a number of following inter-related factors:

1. ***History or Historical Factors**: Historical factor = Kashmir Issue Ka Itihas + Mohammad Prophet Ke Soch,* truthful events has already been discussed above; etc play important role on the general attitudes, beliefs, faith, values, and behaviour of the people of a given state. All these make the tradition and customs of a country which further have their own role in making of the political culture of that country. To quote an example, the English people have their own traditions which are based on slow and gradual change. Thus, they have very easily adopted modern attitudes without any disturbance. There is no revolution in England and the English people are more adjustable and conservative in nature. Similarly, the Britishers had colonial rule over India and also had a long association with India so India had learnt the values of parliamentary democracy with two

houses. On the other hand, France saw revolution because the French people had a radical temperament. They changed their constitution a number of times since the French Revolution of 1789. As a result, the people of Algeria and Vietnam learnt the ways of violent revolution from their French masters = Sutel Ved + S.P. Gargotra.

2. **Geographical Factors = Kashmiri Samaj + demographic change + Satanic view of Damaras:** Geography is also an important factor in determining the political culture. England has been protected from the foreign invasion only because of its island. Hence, the British political culture has not been disturbed by the foreigners. The Britishers enjoy harmonious political culture. On the other hand, the vast frontiers of India attracted the foreign invasions and even the foreigners stayed here as a result, India developed the values of secularism, mixed political culture etc.
3. **Socio-economic Factors:** Socio-economic factors are also the determinants of political culture of a country. For example, a predominantly urban industrialised society is a very complex society due to rapid communication, higher educational standard, groups proliferate, active participation in decision-making process etc. all these factors bring change in the political values and beliefs of a political system. In this way, there is continuous change and development in political culture. But on the other hand, one can observe conservative attitudes, beliefs faith and behaviour etc in rural society with predominantly peasant population. The rural society does not accept the change = low profile government exchequer.

Chapter - 9

Political Participation of Dalits = Nam-History

Liberal democratic societies function properly and successfully with the help of active participation of the people in the political system. People show their participation by making the rallies, as process, by casting their votes, involving themselves in the decision-making process etc.

Definitions = Old into New Concept

1. According to International Encyclopaedia of Social Sciences (Vol. XII), "Those voluntary activities by which members of a society share in the selection of rulers and directly or indirectly in the formation of public policy are known as political participation."
2. In the opinion of Almond and Powell, "Political participation can be defined as the involvement of members of the society in the decision-making process of the system."
3. In the opinion of Heinz Eulau, "Political participation is the involvement of the masses in the decision-making process or policy-formulation."
4. Michael Rush and Philip Althoff state, "Political participation is the movement of the individual at various levels in the political system."
5. J.L. Woodword and E. Roper state that political participation is based on following five political activities:

(i) Voting at pols,
(ii) Supporting possible pressure groups by being a member of them,
(iii) Personality communicating directly with legislators = Dalit Family,
(iv) Participating in political party activity and thus acquiring a claim on legislators, and
(v) Engaging in habitual dissemination of political opinions through word-of-mouth communications to other citizens.

6. **The Centre for the Study of Developing Societies** has identified the following five activities as the parts of political participation:
(i) Voting
(ii) Canvassing for candidates
(iii) Getting out voters
(iv) Organisation of meeting and rallies
(v) Participation in processions
(vi) Distribution of pamphlets and campaign literature
(vii) Other campaign activities
(viii) Campaign through associations and groups
(ix) Attending public meetings and rallies
(x) Membership of political parties
(xi) Conducting party leaders in resolving problems, and
(xii) Conduction government official in solving problems.

Various types of Political Participation

The following are some of the important types of political participation:

1. **Direct Political Participation**: When people directly elect their rulers and participate in the decision-making, policy-formulation processes, this type of political participation is

known as direct political participation. It can be seen in direct democracy.

2. **Indirect Political Participation**: When people elect their representatives directly and through them, they take part in the decision-making process, this type is called as indirect political participation. It is found in representative or indirect democracy like India. The representatives are responsible and accountable to the people.
3. **Active Political Participation = Modi, Ghani Meet**: When people actively take part in the political processes, recruitment, elections, electoral politics, party politics, interest and pressure group activities, organising rallies etc. This type is referred as active political participation.
4. **Low or Passive Political Participation = Great Indian Run:** When people are not interested in the political process and they are not completely oriented towards the political system, the political participation is known as low or passive political participation.
5. **Instrumental Political Participation:** When people participate in politics in order to achieve some definite ends, the political participation is identified as instrumental political participation.
6. **Expressive Political Participation = Black Maveli:** When people participate in political for the satisfaction of their feelings, emotions and sentiments or for social services, it is referred as expressive political participation.
7. **Political Participation through Legitimate Means = Dr B.R. Ambedkar Ka Itihas:** When people participate in the political processes through legitimate and constitutional means like involvement in party campaigns, political meetings and demonstrations etc, it is identified as legitimate political participation.
8. **Political Participation through Illegitimate Means**: Participation in politics through violent and unconstitutional means like riots, violent outbursts, destruction of public property, involvement in political violence, electoral

malpractices etc. fall under this category of political participation through illegitimate means + NC + Congress, and others.

On the basis of political participation, the people can also be classified. Woodword and Roper identify four important classes of people:

(i) Very active
(ii) Active
(iii) Inactive
(iv) Very inactive.

The Centre for the Study of Developing Societies has given five-fold classification of citizens on the basis of level of political participation:

(i) **Apathetics** are those citizens who remain away from politics psychologically.
(ii) **Peripheral** are those who cast their votes but have a little interest in politics.
(iii) **Spectators** are those who cast their vote and have interest in politics also. At the same time, they participate in lower levels of politics.
(iv) **Auxiliaries** are those who have a medium level of interest in politics and who take part in some activities of the political processes.
(v) **Politists** are those who have devoted themselves towards politics completely and participate in the struggle for power and always try to remain in power and maintain power.

Robert Dahl has given four categories of citizens on the basis of level of political participation:

1. The Apolitical Stratum
2. The Political Stratum
3. The Power-Seekers
4. The Powerful.

1. **The Apolitical Stratum:** It is constituted by those citizens who are neither concerned nor informed about politics. They are apathetic towards politics and inactive. A large number of citizens are found apathetic towards in politics even in democratic systems. Robert Dahl has given a number of reasons for such kind of nature of citizens towards politics such as feeling of low rewards, lack of real and effective choice, faith in goodness of decisions, lack of faith in self-role, existence of hurdles etc.
2. **The Political Stratum:** It consists of the people who are concerned and informed about politics and active in political and public affairs. They organise political campaigns, rallies, conference, demonstrations, movements etc. They try their best to involve in the process of decision-making and policy-formulation processes.
3. **The Power-Seekers = Dalit Samaj:** The power-seekers are those persons who are very much interested to gain political power. They are politically resourceful persons. They try to seek power in order to get name, fame, respect, affection, wealth, security and popularity etc. They try every plan to remain in power. Hence, they are power-hunger people.
4. **The Powerful = Nam History + Shivdayal Group:** The powerful stratum includes those power-seekers who want to gain more and more power than others. Their participation in politics is high, active and continuous.

Determinants/Factors of Political Participation

The study of political participation involves the following important factors:

1. **Psychological Factors**: Political participation is influenced by the psychological factors like love for power. Many people find politics as the easiest way to enjoy all kinds of power and respect. Moreover, there is no age-limit and qualification to enjoy political power.
2. **Social Factors:** Political participation is determined by the social factors like education, sex, age, caste, religion, language,

region, residence, urban-rural gap and ethnicity etc. Social factors as determination of political participation are different from society to society and country to country e.g. in British politics, role of social status as a determinant of political participation is reflected in the working of the British party system—House of Lords, Privy Council and Monarchy. In developing countries like India, caste, religion, sex and language are the determinant factors of political participation. Indian political participation is based on the caste groups, caste-based politics and caste-based elections in the formation of government.

3. **Political Factors:** Political factors include the nature of the political system, the organisation of the government, nature and organisation of the political parties, nature of mass-media, decentralisation of powers etc. The political system in which the people enjoy the political rights like right to vote, to contest elections, to criticise the government, to form political parties, right to petition, to peaceful demonstration etc. also encourage them to take part in the decision-making process and policy-formulation.
4. **Economic Factors:** Economic factors are also the important determinants of political participation. These are always in the form of economic gains and incentives. The rich always try to find the way to get involved in the political participation indirectly, e.g. the rich involve themselves through sponsoring the political parties etc.
5. **Environmental Factors:** Environmental factors consists of geography, industrialisation, level of technological advancement, demographic features etc. e.g. due to hot climate conditions, people do not participate in political campaign movements etc. On the other hand, hilly people are passive in politics.
6. **Situational Factors:** These factors have also been playing important role in the process of political participation, e.g. the role of Indian National Congress during national movement proved as situational factor after independence

especially popular participation in politics = declining study of the history. Now-a-days, the wave of Development by B.J.P. is an important situational factor for the political participation of Indians.

Chapter - 10

Learning From Politics= Equilibrium Ke Theory

Political socialisation is a sociological concept of politics through which the people of the country learn the political values, attitudes, behaviour and attitudes towards it. It is very closely connected with the concept of political culture. It provides the necessary political knowledge of the political system. It is a process of political learning which transfers from one generation to next generation. Almond considers it as the first input function of a political system = equality base knowledge.

Definitions = Ameesha Patel Ke History + Kushana Period

1. According to Almond and Powell, "Political socialisation is a process by which political cultures are maintained and changed."
2. Robert Levine defines political socialisation as "the means by which individuals acquire motives, habits and values relevant to participation in a political system."
3. Peter H. Merkl defines political socialisation as "acquisition of political attitudes and behaviour patterns by members of a political system or sub-system."
4. Herbert Hyman states, "Political socialisation is the process of induction into the political culture = Lalu Parsad Ka View. Its end product is a set of attitudes, cognitions, value standards and feelings towards the political system, its various roles

and role incumbents. It also includes knowledge of values affecting, and feelings towards the inputs of demands and claims into the system, and its authoritative outputs."

5. Allam R. Ball defines it as "the establishment and development of attitude to beliefs about the political system."
6. Easton and Dennis state it as "those developments and processes by which person acquire political orientations and patterns of behaviour."
7. In the opinion of Rush, "Political socialisation is a process by which an individual becomes acquainted with the political systems which determine his reaction to political phenomenon."
8. According to Austin Renney, "Political socialisation generally means socialisation of masses, the processes by which ordinary people develop their attitudes towards their political system."
9. Dennis Kavanagh writes, "Political socialisation is the term used to describe the process whereby the individual learns and develops orientations to politics."
10. According to Roberta Siegel, "Political socialisation is the gradual learning of the norms, attitudes and behaviour acceptable to the on-going political systems."

Different Types of Political Social Institution

Almond and Powell have given two types of political social institution:

1. Manifest
2. Latent.

1. **Manifest:** According to them, it is manifest or direct when "it involves the explicit communication of information, values or feelings towards political objects." It can be understood as when certain norms, values or feelings towards political system are imposed on the minds of others directly, clearly and manifestly e.g. rights of the citizens, respect for

authority etc. are certain values of the manifest political socialisation in democratic states whereas compulsory courses of Marxism-Leninism in the erstwhile Soviet Union at school level was another example of manifest political socialisation.

2. **Latent:** Latent political socialisation is "the transmission of non-political attitudes which affect attitudes towards analogous roles and objects in the political system." In other words, latent political socialisation is just like the attitude of submission to the authority of the eldest person in a family which makes others to submit to the authority in one political system. It has deep roots and works automatically.

Agents of Political Institution = Rahul Gandhi Ke Khat Rally Mayawati Ke ideology

Political institution is the process through which the values beliefs emotions and attitudes of a political culture are transferred from one generation to another. This process of transformation can be understood with the help of its following agents:

1. **Family = Sudra State of Mind:** The first and the foremost agent of the political agent for the personality development of an individual. It is the first window of the outside world for the children. Whether the children bring up in a joint family system or nuclear family, they learn authority, power structure and decision-making process. At the same time, the family also transmits politics, political values, party loyalty and voting behaviour to the children.
2. **The School or Educational Institutions = Dera Bias:** The second agent of political institution is the school of educational learning. The school transmits a set of social and political values through its morning and evening assembly, curriculum and extra-curricular activities like cultural activities, debates, discussion, quiz-competitions, seminars, symposiums. Moreover, NCC and NSS activities in the educational institutions impart the values of social services and training for good citizens private properity.

3. **Peer Groups:** Peer groups are known as reference or friendly groups. These groups are characterised by the possession of some common factors like age, educational qualification, social status, liking, common habits = vegetarian samaj, etc. These groups exist outside educational institutions. These are the groups in which the people share their feelings and traditional opinions towards the political system; and modify their political opinion with the performance of the political parties or the government. Hence, these peer groups are very important agents of political socialisation where the political ideas and attitudes are changed and exchanged.
4. **Mass-Media:** Mass-media is also one of the most important agents of political socialisation. It consists of radio, television, newspapers, magazines etc. It provides information about the political happenings. It is the regular source of information to the people of a country. It also shapes and influences their political attitudes and beliefs. Lucian Pye writes, "Socialisation through the mass media is the best short run technique available and it is crucial to modernisation."
5. **Direct Contacts with Political System = Lord Russoesho is philosophy + social-contract theory**: Direct contacts with political system are another important agent of political socialisation. People develop direct contacts with political system with the help of political parties, oppositions, pressure and interest groups, speeches of the political leaders etc. These institutions determine their attitudes and beliefs towards politics. The political parties socialise people through political propaganda, election campaign, by recruiting, articulating and aggregating their interests.
6. **Employment Exchange = Dera Bias:** Exchange of opinion at work places is also an important agent of political socialisation. People learn about the attitude of dominance of employers towards the employees and senior-subordinate relationship; authority and command etc. The general strike of the workers for the increase of their wages and conditions

of work and collection bargaining by the workers may exercise strong political influence or powerful socialisation.

7. **Religious Institution = Barnai Dera:** Religious institutions have significant role as an agent of political socialisation. This agent is the most active in India. In many European countries, the role of the Roman Catholic Church remained very influential to impart political attitudes and behaviour especially among women.
8. **Caste = Infinite Knowledge:** In third world countries, caste is also an important agent of political socialisation. The selection of the candidate, voting behaviour of the people, job reservations, category (scheduled castes and tribes) etc. have the caste-basis.
9. **Symbols:** Symbols also play an effective role in the political socialisation. These symbols include the birthdays or martyrdom days of national heroes such as Mahatma Gandhi, Pt. J.L. Nehru, Bhagat Singh, Subhash Chandra Bose, Lala Lajpat Rai etc. the celebration of these days encourage the young generation for national services = Sawach Bharat Abyian = from city to villages.
10. **National Campaigns:** National campaigns also play important role in the political socialisation. To quote an example cleaning up of habitats (Swachh Bharat Abhiyan) in India.

Chapter - 11

Political Upheavals + Horizontal Knowledge = Dalit Concept

The concept of political development is a very important phenomenon for the newly emerged nations of Asia, Africa and Latin America after the World War II. These nations were technologically backward, politically dependent and economically exploited by the Western societies. The desire for development, social reforms and economic growth remained as a part of their struggle for independence. Their aspiration for independence, national dignity and development found a practical basis for the academic concern with modernisation and political development with a Chapter of Manu = Sunga dynasty.

The term '*Political Development*' entered in the lexicon of Political Science in the 1950s = after the death of Dr B.R. Ambedkar when the newly emerging nations began formulating development plans for the socio-economic well-being of their people. Lucian Pye, Almond Verba, David Apter, Leonard Binder, Riggs, Rastow, Huntington, Myron Wiener etc. are the chief exponents of political development.

Concept of Political Development = Advance History of the Dalit Samaj

1. Lucian Pye's view: Lucian W. Pye is among the first batch of writers to explain the concept of political development. In his important work **Aspects of Political Development,** he gives different definitions accepting and rejecting some of them.

I. **Political Development as the Political Prerequisite of Economic Development:** Economists like Paul A. Baran, Ellis, Buchanan, Benjamin Higgins Albert O. Hirschman and Barbara Ward linked political development with economic development + Amrety Sen Ki Kitab = Nobel Prise Winner.

Lucian Pye criticised this concept of political development on the following four grounds:

(a) It had a negative character = Sandhuse Sharma + Kiran Bakashi.

(b) It did not focus on a common set of theoretical consideration.

(c) The prospects for rapid economic development had become exceedingly dim in most of the poor countries.

(d) The people of the underdeveloped countries were more concerned with political development than rate of economic growth.

II. **Political Development as the Politics of Industrial Societies:** Some social theorists like W.W. Rostow are of the opinion that the process of political development is related only to the countries of industrialisation.

He again rejects this definition of political development by arguing that it neglects the role of other factors like threaten the hold of vested interests, an appreciation of the values of orderly legal and administrative procedure, an acknowledgement that the politics is rightfully a mechanism for solving problems and not an end in itself; a stress on welfare programme and acceptance of some form of mass participation = political issue of the U.P. State + PM of the fure government.

III. **Political Development as Political Modernisation:** Some social theorists like Coleman, Karl Deutsch and S.M. Lipset consider political development as a study of developed or Western or industrialised countries.

Pye disagrees with this view because it fails to differentiate between 'Western' and 'modern' concepts. And secondly, it does not take into consideration the historical traditions of the backward or developing countries.

IV. **Political Development as the Operation of Nation State:** Another group of social theorists like K.H. Silvert, Edward A. Shills and William McCord identify political development with the politics of nationalism.

He rejects this view on the ground that nationalism is only a necessary condition but not a sufficient condition to ensure political development.

V. **Political Development as Administrative and Legal Development**: Some writers like Max Weber, Talcott Parson relate political development with legal and administrative orders.

Pye argues that over stressed administration can create imbalances in the polity which may neglect the essential features of political development, e.g., problems of citizenship-training, popular participation.

VI. **Political Development as Mass Mobilisation and Participation**: Writers like Clifford Greetz, Rupert Emerson, Bert F. Hoselitz and Eisenstadt stressed on the role of politically awakened citizens and the behaviour of people in the direction of an expanding popular participation.

Pye believes that mass manipulation brings disastrous effects on politics. Such a view of political development is dangerous emotionally or corrupting demagoguery and allied political parties like CPM, SP., etc.

VII. **Political Development as a Building of Democracy**: Joseph La Palombara and J. Ronald Pennock connect political development with the building of democracy. It inculcates values of a democratic order in the mind of the people. Pye points out for the exclusion of non-democratic states.

VIII. **Political Development as Stability and Orderly Change**: Karl Deutsch and F.W. Riggs emphasis stability as a legitimate link with the concept of political development. But for Pye, stability also leads to stagnation and political development calls for a somewhat more positive action.

IX. Political Development as Mobilisation of Power: James S. Coleman, Gabriel A. Almond and Talcott Parsons evaluate political development in terms of degree of absolute power in which the system is able to mobilise.

He criticises this concept on the ground that such explanation is applicable to the case of a democratic political system and ignores the case of development in others where the mobilisation of power is deliberately kept limited.

X. Political Development as One Aspect of a Multi-Dimensional Process of Social Change = Computer Age Ke Study: Max F. Millikan, Donald L.M. Blackmer and Daniel Lerner consider political development as one aspect of a multi-dimensional process of social change.

Pye appreciates all forms of development. Development is much the same as modernisation and it takes place within a historical context in which influences from outside the society impinge on the process of social change.

XI. Political Development as Sense of National Respect in International Sphere = Ghai Family Ke Kitab: Some writers consider development as a sense of national respect and dignity in international sphere. Pye says nothing about it. He neither accepts nor rejects it = Jalandhar Baradri.

After analysing different definitions, he has given three characteristics of political development:

(i) Equality

(ii) Capacity

(iii) Differentiation.

(i) Equality: Equality as first important characteristic of political development involves mass participation and popular involvement in the political activities.

(ii) Capacity: It refers to the capacity of political system. It is also closely associated with governmental performance and the conditions that affect such performance. It also defines as effectiveness and efficiency in the execution of public policy.

(iii) **Differentiation:** It means diffusion and specialisation of structures. It also involves the integration of complex structures and processes.

Future Concepts of Political Development

2. **Samuel P. Huntington Political Decay:** Samuel P. Huntington, in his important works like Political Order in Changing Societies and his famous article "*Political Development*", = Sudra Samaj has introduced political development as political decay. He argues that Chinese, Indian, Greek and Egyptian civilisations had highly developed political systems in ancient times but later on, there was political decay in these societies.

3. **Eisenstadt's-Political Development as Political Breakdown:** Eisenstadt has expressed his view on political development in his important essay on '*Breakdown of Modernisation*'. He is of the opinion that the developing countries set up Western type of institutions shifted in North India = J&K State, and refined procedures of work for their modernisation. They believe that these Western institutions would help them in the process of modernisation but in reality, the most of the developing countries are not able to provide institutional framework that can absorb these changes. Hence, it leads to political breakdown.

4. **David Apter:** David Apter has given different stages for political development. Each stage consists of different problems and there is need of control the problems. His developmental stages can be divided into two:

(i) Pre-Industrial Stage
(ii) Post-Industrial Stage.

(i) **Pre-Industrial Stage:** There is need of organised political system to maintain a high-degree control and cohension as a way to industrialisation.

(ii) **Post-Industrial Stage:** There is need of increasing generation and use of new knowledge in this post-industrial stage. Devolution of authority, great decentralisation of high-control systems, reducing direct government control, a non-coercive and high information system etc. play significant roles in the post-industrial societies.

5. Riggs views on Political Development: For Riggs, political development is represented as a kind of dialectical relationship between the process and forces of capacity and equality. There is demand for equality with the growing process of differentiation. There can be no political development, unless movement towards equality is accompanied by the capacity of the system to integrate the system.

6. Leonard Binder's View: Political Development as 'Changes': Leonard Binder has related political development as "changes" in the types and style of politics in his important work **Crisis and Sequences in Political Development.** He explains the syndrome of modernity with the help of three concepts of equality, capacity and differentiation. The following are five characteristics of Political Development as given by Leonard Binder:

(i) Change of identity from the religious to the ethnic and from the parochial to the social.

(ii) Change in legitimacy from transcendental to immanent sources.

(iii) Change in political participation from elite to mass and from family to group.

(iv) Change of distribution from status and privilege to achievement.

(v) Change in the degree of administrative and legal penetration into social structure and out of the remote regions of country.

7. James and Coleman's View: Development Syndrome: Coleman defines political development as a process which involves a continuous interaction among the process of structural differentiation, the imperative of equality and the integrative response and adaptive capacity of political systems. The interaction of these three dimensions is called as the "*Development Syndrome*." = Equality base Knowledge.

8. Kenneth Organski's View: Organski is of the opinion that the treatment of economic development is the most essential in order to study the developing societies. He has given four important stages to pass through before reaching goals of development:

(i) **Political unification,** designed to achieve a centralisation of power in the hands of the state.

(ii) **Industrialisation,** with a view to bring about economic development.

(iii) **National Welfare,** where the result of political and economic power gained by the state, is available to the masses; and

(iv) **Abundance,** where people begin to achieve high standards material affluence.

He is in the favour of economic development whether through Bourgeois system (as in the West), communist methods (erstwhile U.S.S.R, China) or by following Nazi approach = Gandhian history + Hinduism.

9. Walt W. Rostow's View: In his book Stages of Economic Growth: A non-Communist Manifesto, has mentioned six stages of Political Development.

These are-

(i) Traditional stage

(ii) Pre-condition to take off stage

(iii) Take off stage

(iv) Drive towards maturity

(v) Age of high mass consumption

(vi) The search for quality.

Chapter - 12

Democratic Regime=Raj-Rishi Ka Rule

Introduction

Democracy is that form of government in which every citizen enjoys rights, liberty, equality, justice etc. The people are free to express their views. They are free to protest against the government. Constitution is the Supreme Law and independent and impartial judiciary play its role effectively. It is both a form of government and an ideal, an aspiration and a standard.

Meaning and Definitions of the Alert Democracy

Etymological Meaning:

1. The word Democracy has been derived from two Greek words-'demos' and 'kratos' which means 'people' and 'power', i.e. power of the people. = Raj-Rishi Ke Sabita.
2. According to J.S. Mill, "Democracy is the form of government in which the whole people or some numerous portion of them, exercise the governing power through deputies periodically elected by themselves."
3. Sir John Seeley defines it as "a government in which everyone has a share."
4. O.K. Chesterton, "Democracy is, in its essence, a government which is in accordance with the general will of the governed."
5. According to Barker, "Democracy is a mode of spirit, an attitude of mind of those who profess it and those who profess it alone can practice it."

6. According to Hall, "Democracy is that form of political organisation in which public opinion has control."
7. According to American President Abraham Lincoln, "Democracy is the government of the people, by the people and for the people."
8. According to C.B. Macpherson, "Democracy is merely a mechanism for choosing and authorising government or in some other way getting laws and political decisions made."
9. In the words of Professor Dicey, "Democracy is a form of government in which the governing body is a comparatively large fraction of the entire nation."
10. In the opinion of Gettell, "Democracy is that form of government in which the mass of the population possesses the right to share in the exercise of the sovereign power." = Dalit State of Mind Theory.

Evolution of Democracy = Mature Culture

The term '*democracy*' is as old as politics and state. It has a long tradition. Its origin has been traced from the Greek words 'demos' and 'kratos' i.e. the power of the people. Demos originally referred to common people with little or no economic independence. These people were not slaves, but politically illiterate citizens. They were unable to participate in the political affairs of the state. Therefore, they began to pursue their own interests in politics in their own way.

During the fifth and fourth centuries B.C., these citizens were forced to enter into city politics. This kind of transformation has not been fully investigated. But the concept of democracy was very important which reflected under the banner of isonomia-equality before the law, or equality through the law. Thus, democracy was the result of the popular control.

Democracy in Athens- based on lottery system- was criticised by Socrates, Plato and Aristotle. For Plato, democracy was the rule of ignorant. Aristotle defined democracy in his classify, government as the corrupt form of government of many.

With the fall of Rome and the coming of the Dark Age in democracy lost its identity. The barons became powerful and the people had no power in the feudal system of medieval Europe.

There was strong opposition for divine rights of the king. Voltaire and Rousseau's new ideas challenged the existing political system. There was a struggle for supremacy between the Staurt Kings and the British Parliament in England. Later on, the parliamentary form of government was established in England.

John Locke was also in the favour of representative government or limited monarchy in which representation to parliament should be fair and equal. The American Declaration of Independence in 1776 and the French Declaration of the Rights of Man provided the world the first written constitution based on the principles of representative government and the principles of equality of man popular sovereignty. Rise of the political party system strengthened the representative government.

In the Twentieth Century, democracy began to flourish throughout the world especially after World War II. Various states independence from the colonial rules and adopted the democratic set up, for example, India.

Various types of Democracy

There are two types of democracy:

(a) Direct Democracy

(b) Indirect Democracy.

(a) Direct Democracy: In this type of democracy, the people directly express their will on public affairs. They assemble at one place and formulate laws in the meeting. Direct democracy was existed in the small city states of ancient Greece. It was also seen in Vajji Sangha during the Buddhist periods in India. It can successfully function only in less populated states. Switzerland is home land of direct democracy now. Direct democracy prevails only four cantons of Switzerland-Appenzell, Uri, Unterwalden and Glarus. The main features of direct democracy in Switzerland are the referendum, initiative and recall.

Direct democracy is further classified into four categories:

1. Referendum
2. Initiative
3. Plebiscite
4. Recall.

1. **Referendum:** Referendum means seeking public opinion on any law or amendment of the constitution. It is further classified into two types:

(a) Compulsory Referendum

(b) Optional Referendum.

(a) Compulsory Referendum: If the majority of the people and the states (cantons) give their consent to amend the constitution, the Federal Assembly has to amend the constitution, referendum becomes compulsory. Thus, it is known as compulsory referendum.

(b) Optional Referendum: The demand for referendum can be put forward by 30,000 citizens or eight cantons for the treaties with a duration of 15 years or for an unlimited period. It will be enforced only after the majority of the cantons and the people have given their consent.

Different views on Democracy

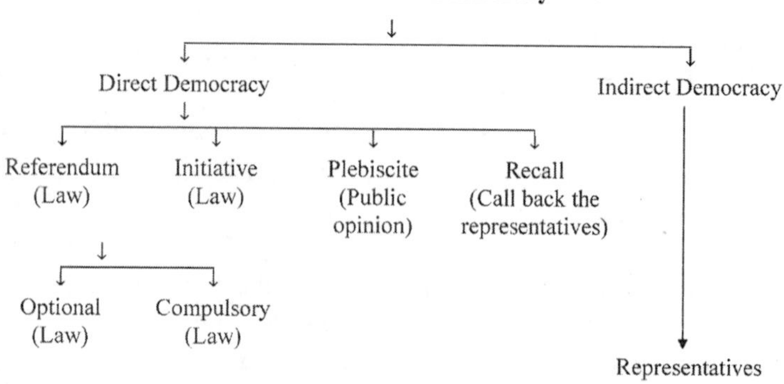

2. **Initiative:** Initiative is another system of direct democracy. Fifty thousand Swiss citizens can send an application to the Federal Assembly for the amendment of the constitution. If the Federal Assembly accepts the resolution, it, at once, starts taking steps to convert into a Bill. If the Federal Assembly rejects it, the proposal is sent for referendum. If the citizens accept it, it becomes the duty of the Federal Assembly to give it the form of a Bill and again send it for the approval of the people and the states. If the proposed Bill is accepted by the majority of the people and the states, it is to be considered as amendment of the constitution.
3. **Plebiscite**: The word plebiscite has been derived from the Latin Word 'Plebiscitum'-which has its origin in two words-Plebis and Scitium. Plebis means people and scitium means decree i.e., people's decree. In other words it means public opinion. It is used only to take the public opinion on political questions and it is not meant for laws.
4. **Recall = Mughal History**: Recall is also one of the important types of direct democracy. The citizens have the right to recall their representatives, if they fail to perform their duties in a proper manner. It reflects the importance and power of the popular sovereignty.

Advantages = Profit base theory of Dogra rulers

1. It is based on the principle of popular sovereignty.
2. It safeguards against majority despotism.
3. There is less chance of revolt.
4. Legislature becomes more responsible.
5. It proves to be the best device to remove a deadlock between two houses of legislature.
6. The people are highly devoted to the state in direct democracy.
7. They take part in the political affairs of the state willingly.
8. They avail the equality of opportunity to serve the state.
9. It encourages patriotism among the citizens.
10. It functions successfully in the small states.

Disadvantages = Rahul Gandhi and Narendra Modi

1. It is unsuitable for large states
2. It is an expensive system.
3. There is possibility of wrong judgement.
4. It may encourage the selfish groups to fulfill their motives.
5. It has no practical utility.

(b) Indirect Democracy: Indirect democracy is also known as representative democracy. In this type of democracy, people elect their representatives. They delegate the power of deliberation and decision-making to their representatives.

Sovereignty lies in the hands of the people in indirect democracy. The government is run on behalf of the people.

Feature of Democratic Regimes

Democracy encourages the personal liberty. The state performs the welfare functions of irrespective of any discrimination. The following are the basic principles or requisites of democracy:

1. **Liberty and Equality:** The democracy is based on liberty and equality. The people enjoy maximum freedom and equality while criticising the system which is only tolerated in democracy. There is no difference among the people on the basis of caste, creed, colour, gender, religion, region, language etc.
2. **Fundamental Rights:** People enjoy fundamental rights. These rights are written in the constitution of the state and granted to its citizens, e.g. the people of India enjoy six fundamental rights.
3. **Independent and Impartial Judiciary:** It is the duty of the judiciary to protect the fundamental rights and other rights of the people. Thus, the independent and impartial judicial system is the most important principle of democracy, e.g., India has Supreme Court and High Courts for the protection of fundamental rights and the constitution.

4. **Independent Press:** It makes a link between the function of government and people. Thus, the mass media should be free from the control of the government.
5. **People Sovereignty:** People are the source of sovereignty in a democracy and the government derives its power from them.
6. **Periodic Election:** There is a provision of periodic election in a democracy so that power should not be concentrated in the hands of a person or a political party. It should be shifted as the people of the state wish.
7. **Universal Adult Franchise:** The people of the State enjoy their basic political right to vote and choose the government of their choices.
8. **Supremacy of the constitution:** The constant Supreme in a democracy.

Criticism = New Discovery

1. Democracy gives more importance to the quantity than quality.
2. Government in democracy may or may not be stable.
3. A huge amount of money is spent in the elections. Hence it is very costly affair.
4. Political parties create unhealthy atmosphere through propaganda.
5. The government in democracy is run by incompetent persons especially in third world countries.
6. Some political Writers like Henry Maine, Lecky etc. criticise it as the greatest obstacle in the progress of culture and civilisation.
7. It proves weak at times of war and crisis.
8. It demoralises the standard of the people.

Theories of Democracy

- Elitist Theory of Democracy
- Pluralist Theory of Democracy

Liberalism gives support to democratic ideas and ideals It has faith in the worth of man and his natural rights. There are three theories of democracy:

1. Classical Liberal Theory of Democracy
2. Elitist Theory of Democracy = Chamar History
3. Pluralist Theory of Democracy.

Elitist Theory of Democracy

Elitist theory of Democracy has developed during the present century. It consists of the institutions of democracy and realities of the Western liberal democratic political system. It gives an interpretation and justification of the existing political systems in the Western democracies.

Meaning and Definitions

The term 'elite' means 'chosen few' in the population = Dalit Historian. Elite consists of those persons who come at the top due to their superior quality. The elites exist in all sectors of the society.

1. According to Laswell, "Elites are the power holders of a body politics." They are, "the holders of a high position in a given society."
2. In the words of C. Wright Mills, "Elites are those who hold the leading position in the strategic hierarchies." + Social Idology.
3. According to Pareto, "Elite consists of those successful persons who rise to top in every occupation and stratum of society; there is an elite of lawyers, an elite of mechanics and even an elite of thieves."
4. In the opinion of Michels, "Elite consists of those few persons who are able to control the apathetic, indolent and slavish people who are susceptible to flattering and obsequious in the presence of strength."
5. According to Suzanne Keller, "Elites are those minorities which are set apart from the rest of society by their pre-eminence in one or more of those various distributions."

6. Presthus defines elites as "minorities of specialised leaders who enjoy disproportionate amounts of power in community affairs."
7. Hunter Commission states, "Those who enjoy reputation for leadership in society and in the eyes of the community, religion, business, various committees, legislature, civic bodies and who are in the real policy-makers are the elite."

The study of the Elite came into existence in the writings of two Italian sociologists Vilfredo Pareto and Gaetano Mosca.

Elitist Theory of Democracy by Pareto

Vilfredo Pareto explained the elite theory of democracy in his famous book *The Mind and Society* (1915-1919). He put emphasis on general social analysis and the study of social problems. He advocates that the society is constituted by the individuals of superior and inferior abilities. The class having superior ability constitutes the elite.

Division of the Society

Pareto divides the society into two stratums:

(a) The higher stratum-Elite

(b) The Lower Stratum - masses and non-elite.

He further divides higher stratum into two categories:

1. Social Elite
2. Governing Elite.

1. Social Elite: It includes successful businessmen, artists, politicians, lawyers, engineers, doctors, teachers' etc. = Dalit History.

2. Governing Elite: It is a small group of individuals who have succeeded and exercise political power.

Division of Governing Elite

Pareto again sub-divides the governing elites into two categories:

(i) The Governing Elite

(ii) The Non-Governing Elite.

Types of Individuals

For him, every society has two types of individuals-Foxes and Lions. Foxes are bold and courageous. They use their cunningness to survive. Whereas lions are strong, brave, conservative, tradition-loving, orthodox and loyal to the ideals of family, religion and country. Hence, they prefer to use force and not cleverness and cunningness. They show interest in stable income from rent. Only these two types of individuals form the government.

Pareto is interested in the nature of the governing elite. For him, the governing elite consists of the top leaders of the political parties. Their power is based partly on force and partly on consent. Here, force plays a leading role in politics. The governing elites always use bribery, deceit and cunningness in order to receive the consent of the masses.

Residues (Qualities)

1. Persistence of aggregates
2. Sociability
3. Activity
4. Integrity
5. Sex
6. Instinct of combinations

Elitist Theory of Pareto = Dalit History + Chura Thought

↓

Stratum

Socia

ning

;)

↓ ↓

Lions Fox

(Circulation of Elites) = U.P. State

of mine

Circulation of the Elite + Jalandhar Rani Didi Ke Soch

Pareto propounds the law of the circulation of elites in history. He states, "History is a graveyard of aristocracies." There is a continuous and regular change of ruling classes from time to time. Thus, there is no stable or permanent political system. Old elites are always replaced by new elites.

Pareto's Concept of Residues = Kala Jadu of Kashmir

He is of the opinion that elites have certain kind of qualities on the basis of which they rise and rule over the state. He identifies these qualities as 'residues'. He has given following six types of residues:

(i) Persistence of aggregates
(ii) Sociability
(iii) Activity
(iv) Integrity
(v) Sex
(vi) Instinct of combinations.

He gives the greatest importance to first and last residues.

Elitist Theory of Democracy by Gaetano Mosca + Hitler Ka View

Mosca has propounded the elitist theory of democracy in his famous work *The Ruling Class* (1939). He has given a theory of elite and circulation of elite. He rejects Aristotle's three-fold typology of government—Monarchy Aristocracy and Democracy. He is the strong supporter of only one kind of government i.e. Oligarchy.

Universality of Elite Rule = Juta Society

Mosca has divided the society into two classes - a class that rules and another class i.e. ruled. The ruling class i.e. elite always in minority but it performs all political functions and monopolies power. On the other hand, ruled class (masses) is in majority. It is directed and controlled by the ruling class. He states, "The larger = Dalit Samaj

+ OBC as the political community, the smaller will be the proportion of the governing minority to the majority to be governed by, and the more difficult, it will be for the majority to organise for reaction against the minority."

Elite - a group of able minority forms Oligarchy

He believes in Oligarchy formed by elites. He states that the majority of human beings accept the domination of a small minority of the society. It leads towards Oligarchy. An active and organised minority (Elite) rules over the passive and unorganised majority i.e. Masses. For him, "The most distinguishing characteristic of the elite is the aptitude to command and to exercise political control."

Circulation of Elites

Like Pareto, he also believes in the circulation of the elites. Old members belong to elite groups are replaced by the new ones. Sometimes, the whole set is replaced by another through a revolution. Once the ruling class loses the aptitude of command and exercising political control, there is possibility of revolution and replacement of the old ruling class by the new ones. Thus, he advises the governing elite to bring about gradual changes in the political system in order to make it sure to mould the public opinion.

Criticism = New Discovery

The elitist theory of democracy can be criticised on the following groups:

1. Elite cannot control the whole sphere of political activities.
2. It is wrong belief that wealthy persons may rise to political power and political structure.
3. Elites are more interested in their personal benefits. They have least interest for the whole community.
4. It ignores the role of political participation in politics.
5. It does not recognise the ability of the masses.
6. It leads towards Oligarchy.
7. It reflects conservatism.

8. It is based on inequality.
9. This theory does not take into consideration the sovereignty of the people.
10. It rejects the principle of responsibility and accountability of the rulers towards the masses.
11. It does not give importance to ideologies.
12. It overemphasises on leaders.
13. It rejects the principles of social and political equality.
14. It is very dangerous for the stability of the democratic political system.
15. It encourages the centralised bureaucratic power.

Pluralist Theory = Women History of Democracy by H.J. Laski

Pluralism is a powerful protest against the monistic theory of sovereignty = Dalit Samaj Ke History + Women Quota which is based on unlimited power. The Pluralist theory originated in the writings of Otto V. Gierke. It began in the last quarters of the nineteenth century and developed in the beginning of the twentieth century. Its traces can be seen in the medieval era where the organisation of state in Europe was loose and the Church, Vocational associations and Guilds played their important role in the society. Reduction of the powers of the state, co-operation between state and other associations, emphasis on welfare state etc. factors are responsible for the rise of pluralism. The chief exponents of pluralist theory are Otto V. Gierke, Maitland, Figgis, G.D.H. Cole, Lindsay, Ernest Barker, Krabbe, Duguit, Cober, Durkheim, H J. Laski etc.

Laski's Views on Pluralistic Theory of Democracy

Harold Joseph Laski was an eminent teacher, political scientist and the British Labour party leader. He was a strong supporter of human liberty and deadly against absolutism and capitalism.

Laski's Important Works

The Problem of Sovereignty = open mind of book, Authority in the Modern State, the Foundation of Sovereignty, A Grammar of Politics, Communism, Democracy in Crisis, The State in Theory and

Practice, The Rise of European Liberalism, Reflections on the Revolution of Our Time, The American Democracy.

Professor H.J. Laski-Pluralist Theory of Sovereignty

Professor H.J. Laski is one of the most important advocates of pluralist theory of sovereignty. He develops his idea about this theory after studying the philosophy of Gierke, Maitland, Figgis, Ernest Barker etc. He combines liberalism and socialism and gives a new idea of democratisation and decentralisation of power in the state. *'A Grammar of Politics: An Introduction to Polities'*, and *'Studies in Law and Politics'* are his some of important works = Encyclopedia of untouchables.

Pluralist Theory of Sovereignty: Laski starts his theory of sovereignty by criticising Austin's Theory of Sovereignty on three ground i.e. historically untrue, legally fictitious and politically unsound. He raises objection on the moral validity of legal theory. For him, the idea of absolute sovereignty cannot function properly especially in federal form of government.

1. **Important Role of Groups = Reserve Race and Association with Mayawati:** Laski gives importance to groups and associations. Individuals form groups and associations according to their need and requirements; likings and disliking, age factors etc. These groups and associations may have social, economic, political, professional, recreational basis. Thus, he pleads for complete autonomy for all groups and associations.
2. **State = J and K and Ladakh as one among various other groups and association = BJP Ke State:** All groups and associations are constituted or found in a state as a part of state so he considers state as one among various other groups and associations. The state is one of them and no one of them is superior to the other = J and K.
3. **First Among Equals:** He is of the opinion that groups and associations grow naturally. They are not under the control of state. They work for their members and compete with the state. Thus, they must have the right to grow as the state

itself. But the priority should be given to the state because it maintains law and order and provides peace. Thus, state is first among equals.

4. **Decentralisation of Power:** He is in the favour of decentralisation of power between state and, its association.

Federal Authority

Federal authority is the central theme of his pluralist theory of sovereignty.

Criticism

1. Sovereignty of the state cannot be divided between state and its associations.
2. It cannot be limited by breaking the class structure of the society.
3. Unity and integration cannot be maintained in the state if there is division of sovereignty among various associations.
4. It leads towards political anarchy and social instability.
5. State may be failed to maintain the rights of individuals and association.
6. No state properly functions under the pressure of various associations and groups.

To sum up, sovereignty is the most important element of the state. With the help of sovereignty, state functions properly and freely and becomes welfare state = Dalit King Ashoka Ke Policy + Damara State of Mind = A.K. Angurana Ke Soch.

Chapter - 13

Authoritarian Regime= Raj-Rishi Ke Sabita

Authoritarian regime is also one of the forms of government in which power lies in the hands of a single person or a group of persons. The people are not allowed to participate in the political affairs of the state. Due to the centralisation of power, even the mass-media is under the control of the government. Thus, authoritarian political system is opposite to the liberal democratic political system.

Authoritarian regime appeared as new form of government in most of the countries in Asia and Africa after World War II. In this form of government, the dictators or rulers exercised their authority with constitutional process. They explain their rise to power to inexorable circumstances. They cultivated in the minds of people that the earlier regimes had corrupted and demoralised. Hence, they promised to restore the democracy. In this way, the present day dictators make democracy an umbrella shelter their authoritarian regimes.

Meaning and Definitions = Future Concept

1. In the words of A.R. Ball, "The states which do not fall in the two categories - Liberal Democracy and Totalitarian state - belong to the category of the Authoritarian state".
2. Baba G.S. Dillon defines it as one in which "all authority and power are concentrated in the hands of a few i.e. the government, whose rule is essentially not responsible.

The people participate in few of their decision but are subjects to all of them".

3. According to E.B. Schulz, "An authoritarian government is characterised by the possession of supreme authority either by one person or by a minority group which is in no way accountable to the people over whom control is exercised."
4. According to Dictionary of Political Science edited by Joseph Dunner, "Authoritarianism is supreme authority = Raj-Rishi Ke Soch as one person or a group of persons without being responsible to people under control. No legal and orderly method of terminating functions, short of forceful overthrow."

Features of Authoritarian Regime = Dr Shabnam Grewal + Others

Authoritarian regime is also equal to dictatorship. Alfred Cobbon has given the following features:

1. One man's rule.
2. Based on force or consent or a mixture of both.
3. Dictator is not responsible to any other authority.
4. He enjoys absolute powers.
5. He runs the administration authoritatively and not according to law.
6. His tenure is not fixed.

Another important feature of authoritarian regimes is given, below:

1. **One Party Rule:** Authoritarian regime is based on one party rule. It believes in one party, one leader and one programme. All other parties are not allowed to function.
2. **No Individual Liberty:** People are deprived of individual liberty. Liberty lies in the obedience to the commands of the dictator. The people do not have freedom of speech, press or association.

3. **Controlled Media:** All the means of communication are controlled by the state or ruler. Any kind of criticism is not tolerated.
4. **Emphasis on Duties:** Authoritarian regime gives importance to duties and not to the rights of the citizens. The people are directed to act on the principle of duty, discipline and sacrifice. Thus, the state is an end and not a means.
5. **Centralisation of Power**: Power is centralised in the hands of dictator or ruler.
6. **Glorifying War = Chandwar:** The dictator or ruler justifies war on authoritarian regime. According to Hitler, "In eternal warfare mankind has become great; in eternal peace it will be ruined." In the words of Mussolini, "War is to the man what maternity is to the woman. I do not believe in perpetual peace; not only do I not believe in it, but I find it depressing and a negation of all the fundamental virtues of man".
7. **Supremacy of the Nation**: Nation is considered as supreme in the authoritarian regime. As Hitler was of the opinion that the Germans were the superior people. Mussolini had also the similar opinion about the Italians. The main objective behind it was to create a sense of superiority among people and prepare them for wars.
8. **Believe in Violence and Force:** Dictators are the strong supporters of violence and force. They feel pride to conquer the neighbouring weak states and extend the boundaries of their states. For example, Hitler conquered Czechoslovakia. Austria, Poland, Belgium and France and enhanced his prestige.
9. **No Opposition:** Opposition parties cannot allow to exist in the authoritarian regime. They are suppressed by the ruler. For example, in Pakistan, ban on the opposition parties has been lifted recently and a democratic government has been installed in Pakistan.
10. **Reject the International Public Opinion:** The rulers do not bother about the international public opinion. They give importance to their own selfish motives and interests, e.g.

Hitler invaded many neighbouring countries without taking into consideration the international public opinion = Bangotra Family Ka Kumba of Nazla Chack.

Advantages = Dalit Theory

1. It establishes a strong and powerful government at the centre.
2. It provides stable and efficient government because there is no periodic election. The ruler enjoys unlimited powers of the government.
3. It encourages economic development as it experienced from Hitler and Mussolini's regimes. Both made special efforts to bring about industrial peace and established Industrial= labour concept + modern discussions found in courts for the settlement of disputes between the capitalists and wages for the workers for violating industrial laws.
4. It is very useful to bring social reforms in the country.
5. It encourages the feeling of patriotism.
6. The dictators face any kind of crisis boldly because powers are so centralised that they can take decision quickly. And decisions are implemented without any delay.

Criticism = New State of Mind

Authoritarian regimes can be criticised on the following grounds:

1. It is against the concept of democracy.
2. It does not provide rights and liberties to the people.
3. It leads the country towards war.
4. It encourages violence and force.
5. No emphasis is attached to the individuals.
6. There is possibility of rebellion and revolution in the authoritarian regime.

Chapter - 14

Theories of Presentation of Sudra in Parliament and State = New Concept

Election plays a very important role for the survival of democracy in the country. The democracy exists with the help of the representations of the people. The following are three important theories of representation in a democratic state:

1. Territorial Representation = Kashmir Teacher on appointments of=SC/ST.
2. Proportional Representation.
3. Functional Representation.

1. Territorial Representation: The territorial representation is also called as geographical representation. In this system, the whole area is divided into a number of electoral districts. These electoral districts are termed as 'Constituencies'. The constituency may be either single-member or multi-member.

(i) **Single Member Constituency:** In this system, one representative is elected from each constituency is called as Single-Member Constituency. A number of candidates can contest election from a constituency. Each voter is allowed to cast one vote through Electronic Voting Machines (EVM-India). A candidate, who secures maximum votes, is declared elected. Single-member constituencies are formed on the basis of small geographical areas, usually equal in population to each other and sometimes identical with political divisions of the country e.g. India, France, Norway and Switzerland.

(ii) Multi-Member Constituency: On the other hand, when the total area is divided into small electoral districts and two or more representatives are elected from each of them, it is known as multi-member constituency.

2. Proportional Representation: The method of proportional representation is based on the principle that the votes should be 'weighted not counted'. The following are the two important methods of proportional representation:

(a) Single Transferable Vote System

(b) List System.

(a) Single Transferable Vote System: It is also known as the Hare System. In this system, the voter is given a paper having names and symbols of all candidates on its left side and blank columns on its right side. The voter has to fill these blank columns with number 1, 2, 3, ... in order to show his order of preferences. He may fill all the columns or some of them, but it is required that the marking of preferences should be done correctly, otherwise his ballot paper shall be declared invalid.

All invalid papers are cancelled during counting and the total number of valid ballot papers is divided by the number of seats to be filled up plus 1, and then the figure of 1 is added to the quotient. This is called electoral quota.

$$\text{Electoral Quota} = \frac{\text{Total number of valid votes}}{\text{Total number of seats} + 1} + 1$$

In India, the members of Rajya Sabha are elected by the members of the State Assemblies in accordance with the system of proportional representative by means of single transferable vote. The election of the President of India is also based on the same system.

(b) List System: In this system, each party is allowed to put up a number of candidates. The names of the candidates of each political party are kept in the separate list; the voter has the choice to cast his vote to any candidate.

3. **Functional Representation = Old democratic concept of Arstotle:** It is based on the occupy composition of the society for the distribution of seats. It means that the doctors should vote for doctors; teachers for teachers miners for miners etc. This system was supported by the Guild socialists also followed in the corporate state of Italy under Mussolini.

It is a reaction against the system of territorial represent and proportional representation. Having an important place in the national legislature, the social, economic and professional groups have encourages functional representation. The idea of functional representation has been taken from the social set up existing in the medieval period when community groups had their autonomous character.

The idea of functional representation had been taken into consideration after World War I e.g. the territorial representation was replaced in Russia by a system based on the vocational principle for the All-Russian Congress in which miners, iron workers, farmers professional men and other classes were allowed to choose their own representatives without regard to territorial representation Mussolini also encouraged the reorganisation of the Italian Senate on the functional basis.

Criticism = New Discovery of the Soul

1. Functional representation makes the legislature an arena of conflicting functional groups. As a result, these groups will not bother about the national interests.
2. It lays more emphasis on the autonomy of the social groups.
3. This system puts unnecessary emphasis on the economic and professional aspects of life.
4. Professor Esmein considers functional representation as "*illusion and false principle which would lead to struggles confusion and even anarchy = Mahajah.*"
5. It leads towards disintegration of nation and encourages a large number of separate communities.

Chapter - 15

Party System = Nuturalism Ke Theory as Old Concept into New Form as History Repeat Itself

Political parties keep the democracy alive in the state. Power to run the government is achieved through the political parties. All the political functions-election to decision, law-making to communication are performed by the political parties. Even the news- through the electronic as well as printed media is the creation of the political parties.

Political party is an organised association of the people having common ideology and faith. It is a group operating to secure the control of a government.

Definitions of Political Party = Dalit-Samaj + Good Human Beings

1. M. Duverger defines political parties as, "groups organised for the purpose of achieving and exercising power within a political system."
2. According to Edmund Burke, "A political party is a body of men united for promoting by their joint endeavours the national interest, upon some particular principle on which they all agree."
3. MacIver defines it as "an association organised in support of some principle of policy which by constitutional means it endeavours to make the determinant of government."

4. In the words of Gilchrist, “A political party is an organised group of citizens who profess to share the same political views and by acting as a political unit tries to control the government.”
5. According to Max Weber, “A political party is a voluntary society of propaganda and agitation, seeking to acquire power in order to procure chances for its active adherents to realise objective aims, or personal advantages or both.”
6. Gettell defines a political party as “a group of citizens, more or less organised, who act as a political unit and who by the use of their voting power aim to control the government and carry out their general policy.
7. According to Jean Blondel, “A political party is a group which is both open in its membership and concerned potentially with the whole spectrum of matters which the polity faces.”
8. Friedrich defines it as “a group consisting of cross-sections of human beings more or less stably organised with the objective in accordance with the condition, of securing or maintaining for its leaders or maintaining for its leaders or maintaining for its leaders the control of a government, and of giving to members of the party, through such control ideal and material benefits and advantages.”
9. Neumann defines it as “the articulate organisation of society’s active political agents, those who are concerned with the control of governmental power and who compete for popular support with another group or groups holding divergent view.”

Important Characteristics of the Political Parties

The following are the important characteristics of the political parties:

1. Agreement on fundamental principles is the most important feature of political parties which bind the people as a political unit.

2. They must be an organised association of people because they have their branches all over the country. Hence, there must be discipline in the parties which can be possible through organisation.
3. They should take into consideration the national interests and not private interests.
4. They must believe in peaceful and constitutional means for capturing the power.
5. The defeated political parties must accept their defeat with grace and start working hard for the next elections.
6. They must have faith in the political campaigns, rallies, ballot-box during elections and not in the use of money and muscle powers for achieving their goals = Brahmin Mat.
7. They must have a good channel of communication with the masses.

Basis of Political Parties

The basis of political parties is different from country to country. The following are the important basis of political parties:

1. **Historical Basis:** History is the base of political parties. With the spread of franchise, it widens the role of political parties, e.g., the National Union of England came into existence as a result of the conditions after the implementation of the First Reform Act of 1832. A.R. Ball has rightly remarked, "Political parties arise when historical changes occur and these are not subject to scientific laws Mahobat Ka Pegam."
2. **Psychological Basis:** Political parties are also based on human nature which gives birth to two types of parties-conservatives and liberals. The persons who do not go in for change but accept the change when it comes, they form conservative political parties. On the other hand the persons who believe in reforms, progress and liberty, they form liberal parties, e.g., the conservative and labour parties of England are based on psychological factors.

3. **Socio-economic Basis:** Socio-economic factors are also responsible for the rise of the political parties. The All India "*Depressed Classes League*" and the *Scheduled Castes* Federation are formed for the betterment of the lot of the Harijans or "*the untouchables*" = one Samaj of the various communities + Sufi Ideology. Some political parties are formed on the basis of religion or culture e.g. the "*Hindu Mahasabha*", the Shiromani Akali Dal, the Muslim League etc. have the religious basis in India. Some political parties have economic base as they support landlordism in the country while another demand for its abolition. Some political parties advocate the policy of nationalisation of all the resources of the country while other may believe in private enterprise.
4. **Ideological basis = Serve the society and study the Vedas:** Some political parties have ideological base e.g. Socialist and Communist parties. These are known as leftist parties because they struggle to change the status quo. On the other hand there are parties based on the 'rightist' ideology as Fascists in Italy, Nazis in Germany and Bharatiya Janata party in India. They stand for the maintenance of the status quo = Idiot Party.

Functions of Political Parties

The political parties perform many important functions in a country. The administrative machinery in democratic government cannot run without the help of political parties. The following are the major functions of the political parties:

1. **Formation of Public Opinion = New Itihas of India:** Political parties play important role in the formation of public opinion by preparing election manifesto, conducting different rallies, door-to-door election campaign etc. They create public opinion in their favour.
2. **Agents of Political Socialisation = Computerised race + Anil Bhagat Ke Sutti from the College**: Political parties are one of the most important agents of political socialisation.

They help in transmitting the values and beliefs of the political system to the people. They provide political education to the people through posters, banners, slogans, meetings etc.

3. **Bridge between the Government and the People = Raj-Rishi Ke Soch:** They act as bridge between the government and the people. They are the important channels of communication for the people to convey their wishes to the government. They highlight the functions of the government through mass-media. In this way, they make the people aware of various policies and programmes.
4. **Role of Opposition = Die down opinion**: They also play significant role of opposition in liberal states. Policies and plans of the government are the product of thoroughly scrutiny conducted by the opposition political parties. Every attempt is made by the opposition to expose the acts of omission and commission of the government. This process makes the government very careful in its works.
5. **Social Welfare Functions = Corrupt State of mind race**: They also performs the social welfare functions inspite of political functions. They work for those people who suffer during the days of famine, draught, epidemic, floods, war etc. They also work for the removal of social evils from the society like illiteracy, untouchability, ignorance, disease etc.= Luta disease.

Types of Party-system

There are mainly three types of party-system:

1. One Party System
2. Bi-party System
3. Multi-party System = New Discovery = Aap.

1. One Party System = Impossible Government: It is also known as single party system. In this system, only one political party enjoys the political power. The people have limited choice to elect one candidate among the different candidates of the same political party.

According to Curtis, "Single party system is characterised by the party in power either dominating all other groups, trying to absorb the political opposition, or in the extreme case suppressing all opposition groups which are regarded as counter-revolutionary or subversive of the regime as forces dividing the national will".

On the basis of Curtis's definition, the single party system can be sub-divided into two categories:

(a) Totalitarian single party system

(b) Democratic single party system.

(a) Totalitarian Single Party System: In this system, the party does not allow other political parties or groups to exist or act as opposition e.g. the Fascist party of Italy under Mussolini and the Nazi party in Germany *under Hitler constituted the totalitarian single party system.* The overthrow of the Czarist system in 1917 is another example of single party system. Now at present, the single party system is existing in China i.e., Communist Party of China.

(b) Democratic Single Party System: A system where the single party allows other parties to function and maintains its dominance, is known as democratic single party system. It can be further classified into three sub-categories:

(i) One-plus single party system

(ii) One dominant party

(iii) One absorbing party system.

(i) **One-Plus Single Party System:** It is the system where the dominant party seldom takes the help of some other political parties, e.g. Liberal Democratic Party of Japan till 2009.

(ii) **One-Dominant Party = Dalit Samaj + Guru Ke Seva:** It is the system where a number of political parties exist but only a single party enjoys a dominant position, e.g. Indian National Congress enjoyed this position till 1967 and soon.

(iii) **One-Absorbing Party:** It is the system where one party absorbs all major and minor political organisations within its fold. e.g. Institutional Revolutionary Party of Mexico,

Kenya African National Union (KANU) of Kenya and National Renovating Alliance of Brazil = New Discovery of pure State of mind people.

Merits of One Party System

1. It saves money and time so the government becomes strong and stable.
2. The state functions properly without ally opposition and criticism.
3. There is no wastage of energy in fighting elections.
4. There is military discipline in the country.
5. It makes the nation progressive within limited time.
6. It gives efficient administration.
7. It gives stable government.

Demerits = Sufi Ideology + Dhamma Policy of Dr B.R. Ambedkar

1. It is against the principles of democracy because people do not enjoy rights, liberty, freedom of thought, expression etc.
2. It destroys the individual personality.
3. There is no freedom of press.
4. It leads towards dictatorship.
5. There is no scope for people to organise them groups for the realisation of their interests.
6. People are bound to obey the orders of the state.
7. It is based on force and fear.
8. Agitations or movements are not tolerated by this system.
9. The election system is mere an eye-wash in this system.

2. Bi-Party System: Bi-party system is also known as two-party system. It is the system where there are only two strong parties which take part in the struggle for power. It does not mean that other parties are not allowed to exist. They may exist but the political power remains between the two major parties in bi-party system, the two major parties share power alternatively. Sometimes, the minor parties

Political Party System

↓

party
em
ition)

Total
Singl
Sy

↓ ↓ ↓

One-plus Single Party System | One Dominant Party System | One Absorbing Party System

may also get the chance to share *power with* either of the two major political parties. It is known as 'two plus' party system. England has bi-party system namely, The conservative and the Labour Party. America has also bi-party system consisting of the Democrats and the Republicans. Belgium, Ireland, Luxembourg also have bi-party systems.

Advantages of Bi-party system: Bi-party system has the following important advantages:

1. The government is strong and stable under this system.
2. The citizens have limited choice to select their representatives.
3. The government can follow a definite policy.
4. The formation of government is very easy.
5. The opposition party is strong and is always ready to expose the shortcomings of the party in power.
6. Discussion can be carried on in this system.
7. Under the bi-party system, the members of the electorate face with only two alternative issues.

Disadvantages = Brahmin Samaj Ko: Bio-party system has the following important is advantages:

1. People do not have enough of choice.
2. It puts limitation on the public opinion.
3. It gives rise to cabinet dictatorship.
4. The party members do not have freedom of opinion in this system.
5. This system divides the whole nation into two groups.
6. The government is backed by a solid majority in the legislature under this system.

3. Multi-party system: A number of political parties exists in a political system is known as multiparty system. In this system, when no single party is in a position to form the government, several parties form a coalition to run the government. Moreover, national political parties and regional political parties are found in this system. Regional political parties take more advantages in the formation of the government in countries like India. Italy, Switzerland and France also have the multi-party system. There is lack of political stability in the system.

Advantages = Political Monges

1. The members of the political parties enjoy freedom of opinion in this system.
2. The people have unlimited choice.
3. It is based on the democratic ideals. Thus, it allows every opinion.
4. It is more elastic than other system.
5. MacIver remarks, "Under this system, groups can be feely organised, can unite and separate with every change of the situation. Opinion-groups, being liberated from a common organisation, are able to formulate their doctrines without compromise."
6. Nation is not divided into two groups.
7. Legislature controls the executive in this multiparty system.

8. Different opinions are represented in the legislature through this system.

Disadvantages = Brahminmat

1. The formation of government is very difficult in this system.
2. There is possibility of political instability.
3. Election in this system is a costly affair.
4. It cannot continue any policy due to the change in the government.
5. Coalition makes the government weak and inefficient.
6. Even the minor difference of opinion among the coalition partners will lead towards the break-up of the coalition government.
7. There is lack of strong opposition.
8. It does not provide party discipline among the legislators = Dera Bias Ke Soch.

Chapter - 16

Globalisation + Chamar thought = Dogra Imperialism

Globalisation is the latest development of post-cold war and the collapse of Russia in international relations. Globalisation is the process of integration of world's economies in conditions of free flows of trade and capital and movements of persons throughout the world. It is facilitated by new technologies for instant communication of information. It is a process of growing interdependence between the people of all nations. The phenomenon of globalisation has captured the attention of the world in the field_s of information superhighway, international trade, telecommunication internet etc. Globalisation is a socio-economic process which has lessened the territorial distances and made the socio-economic and cultural arrangements for further developments.

Definitions

1. The International Monetary Fund (IMF) described it in 1997 as, "the increasingly close international integration of markets both for goods and services, and for capital."
2. Again according to the International Monetary Fund, "Globalisation is characterised by increase in flow of trade capital and information, as well as mobility of individuals, across borders."
3. In the words of Thomas Friedman, "Globalisation is an overarching international system shaping the domestic politics=

Home Rule Movement of Annie Basant and foreign relations of every country through Brahminism = Modi, Ghani Meet Afghanistan. It is also enabling people to share their unique individuality farther and farther = future course of action."

4. In the opinion of S.K. Verma, "Globalisation is primarily a removal of national barriers to trade and investment + Chamar Issue from Ravi to Raj-Rishi. It is associated with contemporary phenomenon of privatisation, de-regulation, the expanded provision of incentives for entrepreneurial behaviour, structural adjustment programmes and related pressures on developing countries to open-up their markets for international financial institutions and developed countries. Globalisation, in economic terms, is the opening up of the markets which will operate under market forces, where state will have a very little role to play."
5. According to Secretary-General of the UNCTAD, Rubens Ricupera, "Globalisation is the integration of the world economy as the result of three main forces:
   (i) Increase in trade in goods and service;
   (ii) The increase in the investment of transnational companies and the consequent change in nature of production;
   (iii) International financial and exchange rate transactions."
6. Anthony Gidden defines it as "The intensification of world wide social relations which link distant localities in such a way that local happenings shaped events occurring many miles away and vice-versa."
7. Herod, Thathail and Roberts remark, "Globalisation is an imperfect name for a differential and uneven process of transition from an international economy to an imaginary unified global economy."
8. According to Baylis and Smith, "Globalisation is the process whereby social relations acquire relatively distance-less and borderless qualities."

9. In the words of Edward S. Herman, "Globalisation is both an active process of corporate expansion across borders and a structure of cross-border facilities and economic linkages that has been steadily growing and changing as the process gathers steam."
10. In the opinion of Robertson, "Globalisation is a concept that refers to the compression of the world and the intensification of the consciousness of the world as a whole."
11. According to Barry Bosworth and Philip H. Gordon, "Globalisation is the expansion and intensification of linkages and flows across borders."
12. According to Scholte, "Globalisation refers to processes by which social relations acquire relatively distanceless and borderless qualities so that human lives increasingly play out in the world as a single place."
13. According to Deepak Nayyar, "Globalisation is a social process associated with increasing economic openness, growing economic independence and deepening economic integration between countries of the world economy."
14. In the words of M. Waters, "Globalisation is a social process to which the constraints of geography and social and cultural arrangements recede and in which people become increasingly aware that they are receding."

Globalisation: Evolution

Though globalisation is a major phenomenon appeared towards the end of twentieth century, its origin can be traced back in the ancient and medieval periods also. The evolution of globalisation can be classified into three categories:

1. Archaic Globalisation = Ancient Greek.
2. Proto-Globalisation = Primitive Greek.
3. Modern Globalisation = Relating to Present Situation.

1. **Archaic Globalisation, Ancient Kandhar, Modern Afghanistan:** Ancient globalised economies and culture are known as archaic globalisation. It existed during the

Hellenistic Age where commercialised urban centres were focused around the axis of the Greek culture. It spread from India to Spain. This kind of trade relations for the first time gave the idea of a cosmopolitan culture.

2. **Proto-Globalisation = Mauryan Civilisation:** Proto-globalisation emerged due to the rise of maritime European empires - the Portuguese and the Spanish Empires in sixteenth century and the Dutch and the British Empires in the seventeenth century. In the seventeenth century, globalisation was a private business phenomenon e.g. The British East India Company, founded in 1600, was the first multinational corporation.

   It was the age of Discovery in which Eurasia and Africa remained engaged in substantial cultural, material and biologic exchange with the New World. Exploratory voyages, discovery of America, establishing of Portuguese factories from Africa to Asia and Brazil, trade of local products like gold, spices, timber etc. are the example of this globalisation= New horizontal opinion of Ashraf Ghani (Afghanistan Ka President).

3. **Modern Globalisation = Chamar thought (*Northlines* p. 6):** Modern globalisation began with the coming of industrialisation in nineteenth century. Imperialism, incorporation of Sub-Saharan African and the Pacific islands into the world system, yielding of valuable natural resources like rubber, diamonds and coal by the Europeans, out-break of World War I and II etc. were the important events of modern globalisation.

Nature of Globalisation = Natural History of Pliny

Globalisation is not a new concept in the field of comparative politics. It is sometimes related with countries or companies and even with the involvement of individuals throughout the world. It is a worldwide phenomenon. By the 1980's this term was commonly used for specifically economic globalisation. It referred to worldwide trade linking economies together and interdependent. Now, it is neither a purely economic process nor is related to communication only. It is a multi-dimensional phenomenon which is enhancing the socio-economic, industrial-trade-cultural relations among the people living in different parts of the globe. It primarily consists of trade, capital investments, movement of the people and spread of information technology. At the same time, it allows other social activities, labour organisers, journalists, academics to work on a global stage. Thus, the impact of globalisation can be observed in all fields so its nature can be understood in the following ways:

1. **Liberalisation:** The policy of liberalisation is the basic nature of globalisation through which the restrictions on international economic transactions are removed. It provides free capital markets which are open to private and foreign enterprises.
2. **Privatisation:** Conducting of majority of economic activities by the private sector is known as privatisation. It provides opportunities of investment to the foreign private investors.
3. **Role of Multi-National Corporations:** Due to liberalisation and privatisation, globalisation encourages the multi-national corporations. These corporations increase production and distribution due to their unique and empirical capacities. Thus, globalisation provides opportunities to MNCs for their expansion.
4. **International Institutions:** Globalisation is boosted flourished by several international institutions like the World Trade Organisation (WTO), the IMF and the World Bank even the UN agencies such as the ILO, the UNDP, the UNCTAD etc. Even series of agreements like General Agreement on Tariffs and Trade (GATT) NIEO etc. have played important role to remove restrictions on free trade.
5. **Flow of Foreign Capital:** It encourages flow of foreign capital in the form of foreign direct investment, commercial borrowing etc. Transfer of capital from developed countries to developing or underdeveloping countries can bring different benefits.
6. **Increase in Technology and Marketing:** With the help of globalisation, the MNCs are making increase in the marketing

services like marketing research, advertisement, spread of marketing information, storage facilities, transport, packing, designs etc.

7. **Increase in Knowledge:** Globalisation provides rapid knowledge to the developing countries. Thus, these countries get a kind of encouragement for their faster growth.
8. **Socio-economic Transformation:** Globalisation is also a socio-economic phenomenon so it has brought drastic change in life-styles of the people of developing and under-developing countries. The good features of Euro-American societies like dignity of labour, responsibility for neighbourhood or community welfare, respect for law and order and respect for knowledge and character etc. are transmitted to developing countries.
9. **Cultural Transformation = Truism Ke Value:** Globalisation has also transformed the Western culture to rest of the world through transnational companies and the emergence of the global commodities like wide spread of satellite communication telecommunication networks, internet, cyber cafe, global media corporations. WhatsApp, U Tube, Home Shopees, Face-book etc. = old concept in New form. Moreover, it has created cultural homogenisation by launching Coca Cola, Pepsi, Uncle Chips, Restaurants like Pizza Huts, McDonald, Domnic or wearing European garments etc., found in the modern generation of India, *Saree* is an old concept of Hindu society = landless statement of Dalit historian = I do not like it.

Chapter - 17

Human Rights = Representative of God

The term human rights is not a new phenomenon in the study of international politics. One of the earliest documents on human rights was the *Magna Carta* which was forced by the English Barons on King John in 1215 = Ganpati Genesh Ke Pooja = Dalit-Megh Brahmin Samaj of U.P. Dr Naval Vijogi, now made residential quarter at Ludhana. Its idea can also be traced in the writings of J.S. Mill, Thomas Paine, Hobbes, Rousseau etc. Moreover, the American Declaration of Independence, the French Declaration of Rights of Man and Citizens etc. are also reflected the concept of human rights.

The killings of millions of Jews by the Nazis in the 1930s and compelled the world to think over the human rights in a systematic way. The formation of United Nations has been landmark in the Institutionalisation of human rights. Human rights are recognised as one of the most important objectives of civilised life after the end of World War-II.

The UN Charter = nil/nil human psychology of the Brahmin Samaj = Megh Baradari = few Idols has represented an important advancementby advocating a firm faith in and respect for Human Rights of all the people living throughout the world. The Preamble to the Charter reaffirms human rights as "faith in fundamental human rights and in the dignity and worth of the human, person, in the equal rights of men and women = Brahminical Mat."

The UN Charter seeks to "Achieve co-operation in promoting and encouraging respect for human rights and for fundamental freedoms for all without distinction as to race, sex, language or religion".

Universal Declaration of Human Rights

UN General Assembly adopted the Universal Declaration of Human Rights on 10th December, 1948. After its establishment, every year, 10th December has been observed as the Human Rights Day all over the world. This declaration consists of one Preamble and 30 Articles which contain civil, political, economic, social and cultural rights.

Meaning of Human Rights = Political View of the Dalit Historian

Human rights can be explained as those basic rights through which every individual can feel as a respectful member of the society irrespective of race, colour, sex, language, religion, region etc. Human rights stand for:

1. Right to life, liberty, dignity and security of a person.
2. Equality before law and equal protection of law.
3. Right to freedom of movement and residence within the borders of each state. Everyone has the right to leave any country, including his own, and to return to his country.
4. Right to recognition, everywhere as a person before the law.
5. Right to a nationality.
6. Right to seek and enjoy in other countries asylum from persecution.
7. Right to freedom of thought, conscience and religion.
8. Right to freedom of opinion, expression; peaceful assembly and association.
9. Right to work, to free choice of employment.
10. Right to rest and leisure.
11. Right to education.
12. Right to freely participate in the cultural life of the community.
13. Prohibition of slavery system.
14. Prohibition of torture or cruel or inhuman or degrading treatment or punishment etc.

Significances of Human Rights = Broad base Knowledge

Human rights are so significant that a number of bodies like Charter-based bodies and eight human rights treaty-based bodies were established

I. Charter-Based Bodies = Karamyogi:

(i) Former Commission on Human Rights

(ii) Human Rights Council

(iii) Universal Periodic Review

(iv) Special Procedures.

(i) **Former Human Rights Commission**: This Commission was established by the UN Economic and Social Council. It was responsible for monitoring human rights protection. It worked between 1946-2006. In 2006, it was replaced by the Human Rights Council.

(ii) **Human Rights Council = Guruji Ke Spirit:** This council is empowered to prevent abuses, inequity and discrimination, to protect the most vulnerable and, to expose the perpetrators.

(iii) **Universal Periodic Review = Ginni Mahi Ka Juta**: Universal periodic review is a process by which a review of the human rights records of all the member states of UN is done once in every four years.

(iv) **Special Procedures = Documentary Proves**: Special procedures constitute the mechanisms to address either specific country situations or thematic issues in all parts of the world. These procedures are either an individual- a special rapporteur or representative of the Secretary General, or an independent expert or a working group. Special procedures consist of two mandates-

(a) Country mandates

(b) Thematic mandates.

(a) **Country Mandates:** These mandates call on mandate-holders to examine, monitor, advice and publically report on human rights, situations in specific countries or territories.

(b) **Thematic Mandates** consist of major phenomena of human rights violations worldwide.

II. Treaty-Based Bodies: The following are eight human rights treaty-based bodies which are committees of independent experts that monitor implementation of the core international human rights treaties:

(i) International Covenant on Civil and Political Rights (ICCPR).

(ii) Committee on Economic, Social and Cultural rights (CESCR).

(iii) Committee on the Elimination of Racial Discrimination (CERD).

(iv) Committee on the Elimination of Discrimination against Women (CEDAW).

(v) Committee against Torture (CAT) and Optional Protocol to the convention against Torture (OPCAT)-Subcommittee on Prevention of Torture.

(vi) Committee on the Rights of the Child (CRC).

(vii) Committee on Migrant Workers (CMW).

(viii) Committee on the Rights of Persons with Disabilities (CRPD).

Human rights treaty-based bodies ensure prosperity, equality and freedom to the people all over the world. These rights prohibit the idea of discrimination on the basis of racial superiority, discrimination against women in public life, education, employment, health, marriage, family etc. These rights also protect the rights of child as primary healthcare and education etc.

Trends of Human Rights = Social Justic Ka Ithas

As already stated the significance of human rights in this contemporary world, like establishment of various charter-based bodies and human rights treaty-based bodies. Human rights contain social, economic, political, natural and basic rights. As the result of its significance and the changing scenario, the following are the important trends of human rights:

1. **Role of International and Regional Human Rights Organisations:** International organisation includes the United Nations Development Programme, the multilateral

institutions exemplified by World Bank, the IMF, World Health Organisation, and the International Labour Organisation (ILO) etc. Regional inter-governmental organisations include Inter-American Commission on Human Rights Organisations of American States; Council or Europe; European Court of Human Rights Organisations for Security and Co-operation in Europe. All these organisations have been working for human rights.

2. **Growing Role of Non-Governmental Organisations**: A number of non-governmental organisations (NGOs) have been playing important role on international human rights issues, Amnesty International, Human Rights Watch, Freedom House, American Civil Liberties union etc. are the important NGOs which actively work on human rights.
3. **Rise of Social International Movements and Normative Regimes:** Human rights gave birth to different social movements and normative regimes such as feminist movements, peace movements, gay/lesbians rights movements, animal rights movements. These movements have brought awareness among the people all over the world about human rights.
4. **Role of Information Technology:** The role of information technology like computer, U Tube, Google, etc. has also an essential tool for the promotion of human rights. Various instruments like the Fax Machine, E-mail, G-mail, the Internet etc. have been playing effective role in the formulation of effective responses to the violations of human rights.
5. **Role of Globalisation:** Globalisation has also promoted the human rights throughout the world.
6. **Human Rights and Terrorism:** Every kind of terrorist activity has international implications in this age of globalisation and interdependence. The fight against terrorism has become more significant after September 11, 2001 attack on World Trade Centre. As Narang has remarked, "Both the acceleration in terrorism and fight against it have

> also brought a major debate on the issue of terrorism and human rights."

Terrorist activities like killing, injury people, destruction of property, deprivating people from their freedom, kidnapping etc. have also been creating a sense of the awareness about violation of human rights. As a result, it proves helpful in creating world public opinion about human rights.

Chapter - 18

Climate Change = No Caste System

The long-term weather trends like seasonal patterns of temperature, rainfall, snowfall and other elements of the weather are called "*climate*" in other sense of the Sufi Ideology called "Socialism". This long-term weather trends consists of 30 years weather conditions. It affects the entire Earth Variations in the behaviour of the weather over long time periods like from one century to another, are known as climate change. Climate variation occurs as a response to "climate forcing" which is the factor that can cause either a warming or cooling of the atmosphere.

The world has been facing climate changes on the earth. One of the most important causes behind it is *'Green House Effect'* = new discovery of the art historian due to excessive emissions of green house gases like Carbon-dioxide, Methane, Nitrous Oxide etc. 'Green House Effect' is leading towards 'Global Warming'. Pollution = Brahmin Samaj, physical changes and deforestation etc. are also responsible for climate changes. Moreover, the global environment has been threatened with the widespread of globalisation, growth of market economy, information technological revolution, means of communication and transportation etc.

The climate changes have brought marked changes in crop-profile, increase in desert lands, changes in bio-diversity melting of icebergs and glaciers resulting in rise of sea level, irregular rainfall, droughts, floods, cyclones etc.

Thus, the climate change and ozone depletion are the two most challenging environmental problems in this contemporary period. The pattern of development followed since the age of industrialisation has caused crisis in the global environment. There are two important aspects of environmental problem:

(i) The environment cannot be divided among countries on the basis of territory.

(ii) The present problem of environment is the climate change which is the cumulative effect of the unsustainable growth pursued for centuries.

By taking into the consideration of climate changes, the first initiative was taken by the international community by helding Stockholm Conference in 1972 on Environment under the auspices of the UN. A number of conferences and summits have been held after that to sensitise the states and world about the environment problems like climate change, global warming, pollution etc.

The modem day industrial and commercial activities are the chief sources of emission of greenhouse gases. The UN Inter-governmental Panel on Climate Change (IPCC) has published various reports on climate change. The world has been facing the problem of crossing 2°C temperature rise over pre-industrial period. The year 1850 is marked as the dividing line between the industrial and pre-industrial period. If the global temperature rises beyond 2°C above the pre-industrial level, severe climate change conditions would result. The IPCC predicted that the global temperature would rise from 1-1°C to 4-6°C by the year 2100 depending upon the efforts of global community to check the greenhouse gases. At present the basic objective of global efforts is to limit the global rise in temperature to 2°C above the 1850 level by adopting measures to put a cap on the global emission of greenhouse gases.

UN Framework Convention on Climate Change (UNFCCC): 1992 = General Opinion

The UN took major step to take appropriate global action to prevent the climate change. This convention aimed at achieving stabilisation of greenhouse gases. It also established a mechanism called Conference of Parties (COP) as the highest decision-making and supervisory body under the convention.

North-South Dialogues

Kyoto Protocol 1997

Third meeting of the conference of Parties to the UN Climate change conservation in Kyoto, Japan adopted the Kyoto Protocol to reduce global emissions of greenhouse gases. Under this Protocol, 37 countries committed themselves to reduce four greenhouse gases-carbon-dioxide, methane, nitrous oxide, sulphur hexafluoride and two groups of gases (Hydro fluorocarbons and perfluorocarbons) produced by them. On the other hand, the low-income group, with a very few classified as middle-income were not obligated by the limits of emissions in the Kyoto Protocol. Even fast growing economy countries like China, India, South Africa and Brazil were kept in this non-obligated group. The agreement aimed to lower overall emissions from a group of six greenhouses gases by 2008-12.

The United Nations Climate Change Conference 2010 = Surat Split Ke History

This conference was held in Cancun, Mexico. It was the 16th Conference of the Parties (COP) and the sixth meeting of the Parties (MOP) to the Kyoto Protocol. The differences between the developing countries and the developed countries could be seen. The developing countries, less developed countries and small island countries wanted to continue their previous positions as non-obligated group. They shifted the historical responsibility of the developed countries for maximum greenhouse emission. They argued that climate change action should be guided by principles of historical responsibility and common and differentiated responsibility. They also wanted the extension and continuation of the Kyoto Protocol which gave some relief to developing countries.

On the other hand, America and the developed countries wanted to replace the Kyoto Protocol. They wanted to make emission of greenhouse gases applicable to poor countries also. At the same time, they also wanted larger emitters like India and China to be more transparent about domestic emission curbing actions.

The Cancun Conference, 2010 was not proved as successful in delivering the goods to the world. The Cancun documents recognised emission targets set by industrialised and developing countries. It requires that the inventories of national emissions are shared annually by industrialised countries and once every two years by the developing countries. The agreements are expected to be transformed into a legal treaty at next December 2011 conference in Durban, South Africa. There is also a pledge of $30 billion fast-start finance from industrialised countries to support climate action in developing countries. The environment groups state that the Cancun Agreement has failed to establish any mechanism to ensure that the industrialised countries did not break the pledges made. Secondly, they have fear about the end of the Kyoto Protocol through the Cancun Agreement. The action of India has been criticised. India has shifted from her earlier position and has given a hint that she would eventually consider legally binding curbs on emissions, which has been viewed as a betrayed. The poor countries have seen this as a keen India to become a part of the global alliance of polluters at the cost of poor countries. Hence, the politics of environment is still continue. There is the North-South Division and the world is divided into haves and have-nots.

Lima Conference of Parties (COP), December 2014, Mass Communication + New Media

The 20th round of the annual climate, change negotiations held in Peru, Lima on December 1-12, 2014 again proved unsuccessful due to the differences between the developing and the developed countries.

196 countries participated in this conference in which India represented the causes of developing countries. India has given the following arguments:

(i) The developed countries should bear the historical responsibility for carbon emission.

(ii) They should also bear the responsibility to provide finance and technology to overcome climate change impacts in the developing countries.

(iii) The developing countries should not be burdened with binding carbon emission in a manner which disturbs their development process.

(iv) India insisted to focus on adaptation aspects of climate change managements.

Here, adaptation aspects mean those steps which enable the developing countries to cope with the harmful impact of climate change. These harmful impacts are already visible in many developing and small Island countries.

On the other hand, the developed countries were in the favour of focusing on mitigation measures. Mitigation measures mean those steps like reduction in carbon emission which eliminate the root causes of climate change crisis.

BASIC

The developing countries have organised under the banner of G-77 and other small groups. However, the four leading developing countries have formed another group called BASIC (Brazil, South Africa, India and China) for putting a common approach in these negotiations. This kind of polarisation led towards deadlock between north and south in the negotiation over many issues. But in order to find consensus on minimum points, more negotiations were advanced for two more days upto December 14, 2014. After many rounds of meetings, the parties agreed on certain minimum points which were included under the final document called as 'Lima call for Climate Action'. This plan paves the way for final binding agreements signed in 2015 Paris, France.

Critical Appraisal = New Vichar

The real problem lies with the persisting differences between the developing and the developed countries on the main issues of these negotiations like adaptation vs mitigation, provision of finance and availability of advanced technology to poor countries and concerns of common but differentiated responsibilities.

Moreover, America and other developed countries do not recognise China and India as developing countries. They term as emerging economies. America wants China and India to bear the equal responsibility like other developed countries. But this responsibility is not acceptable by China and India = Old rivalry groups of North Korea.

Chapter - 19

Women's Issues = Sudra State of Mind

United Nations report states, "Women constitute half of world population, perform nearly two-thirds of work hours, receive one-tenth of world's income and own less than one-hundredth per cent of the world's property." They are oftenly referred as the 'Better half of Men' but in actual life, they have the worst deal at the hands of the society. They have not received the due place in the society. They are denied of their rights. They are considered as second grade citizens in the patriarchy; Discrimination of women from birth to death is well-known. Inequality for them can be observed in an sectors like socio-economic, political, civil liberties, identity, education, healthcare, nutrition and legal sector etc. Thus, a number of issues regarding women can be categories in the following ways:

1. Social issues = Jat-Pat.
2. Economic Issues = Rich and Poor.
3. Political Issues = Dalit History.
4. Health Issues = Sound body + Sound mind.

1. **Social Issues = Jat-pat:** Social issues include gender-based discrimi-nation, crime against sexual assault, or harassment, dowry-demanding, bribe-burning, racial discrimination, hurtful husbands domestic violence, economic inequality, sexual discrimination in education, the workplace and the home, honour killing etc.

Moreover, one more issue can be added as a socio-economic women issue which is linked with the widows living in Vrindavan.

They are compelled to live in pitiable and pathetic conditions due to lack of financial, social and emotional supports of their families. They depend upon 'beggary' which is a social problem of the twenty-first century, old Brahminism converting in Dalit Samaj.

On the other hand, one woman is raped every 22 minutes in India. The Supreme Court of India has recommended compensation for rape survivor, death compensation, compensation for acid attack survivors etc. Two decades ago, the Supreme Court of India has directed every state government to set up a compensation scheme for rape survivors = Pakistani Raffues. The Centre has also allocated crores for this purpose. Even then, the survivors struggle for the financial assistance i.e. owed to them = nalik BJP Govt. failed to resolve the Kashmiri + other financial matter = Jan Dhan Yojana.

2. **Economic Issues = Rich and Poor**: The contribution of women at household is not recognised because it is considered as unpaid work. In the developing countries like India, the women of the lower castes or classes go out for work as labourers. The contractors or capitalists engage them at a very low payment. They are also deprived of property rights and land-owning, abject poverty etc. Women are poor in most of the countries of the world. Women experience extreme poverty with limited access to resources especially in Asia and Africa.

3. **Political Issues = Dalit History**: The women have no proper representation in the central legislature and in all important decision-making bodies though they have been enjoying their political right i.e. right to vote.

As per data, the percentage of women in legislatures in general in some of the countries is as- China and Switzerland (21 per cent), England 18 per cent, Australia 15 per cent, Zimbabwe 14.7 per cent, America 11.7 per cent, France 6.4 per cent and Japan 4.6 per cent. Parliamentary seats occupied by women on average in the world are 11.7 per cent. women are still struggling for 33 per cent reservation in legislature. They have 33 per cent seat reservation in local self-governments i.e. Panchayati Raj system and municipality in India.

4. Health Issues = Sound Body sound Mind: Discrimination against girls and women in the developing world is a devastating reality. Women health issues include malnutrition, poor health, maternal mortality, infanticide, sex-selective abortion or illegal abortion.

Illegal abortions lead to many deaths of women as they are done by unqualified, untrained people in highly unhygienic places. Moreover, abortion is conducted intentionally after knowing the gender of the unborn foetus which is highly illegal. Most of the illegal abortions have taken place due to an urge to have a male child.

Women Empowerment = Economic Development

Empowerment is a kind of atmosphere of help or support to women to achieve equality with men so that the gender discrimination may be removed. Due to various issues and inequality etc. they need to be empowered in all walks of life. In order to fight against the socially constructed gender biases, women have to swim against the stream that requires more strength. Such strength comes from the process of empowerment.

Empowerment is an active multi-dimensional process which enables women to realise their full identity and powers in all spheres of life. They require empowerment because hierarchies of power are dominated by the males so they are unable to raise their voices. Women's empowerment include both a personal strengthening and enhancement of life chances and collective participation in achieving equality of opportunity, freedom of thought, speech and expression equality between different genders etc.

When the term 'empowerment' is used in the society, it reflects that there is a weak class which needs sensitisation and empowerment. Being the weaker sex, they should be empowered through the following ways:

1. Educational Empowerment = Nam.
2. Political Empowerment = Dalit Concept.
3. Socio-Economic Empowerment = Ph.D. in History = story of two great forces God and Man.

1. **Educational Empowerment**: Education can play an important role in empowering women. It can bring awareness among women

about the women rights and laws. It can make empowerment effective if some chapters relating to women rights and law may be kept in the curriculum of social studies at the high school levels.

Thus, education can strengthen their mind and power of thinking. It is said, "When you educated a man, you educate an individual, but when you educate a women, you educate a family and nation."

2. **Political Empowerment:** The term 'empowerment' in political context means the existence of a weak-class in the society which needs sensitisation and freedom which make them enable to participate in social, economic, political and cultural spheres of life.

Political empowerment for women means their role in political participation, political behaviour and actions related to influence the decision-making process and participation in the process of governance.

Moreover, there should be provision of reservation for women in getting political position so that it may enable them to collectively influence and direct the laws, policies and programmes in their favour. Reservation is a way to force women to come out, it may shed their shyness and hesitation and their creative energy will be released to the advantage of the community at large.

3. **Social Empowerment:** Social empowerment of women is directly linked with the social and national development. Their low social status can be improved with the important role of media and socio-political institutions = economic status + education, both "formal" and "informal".

Index

L

M

N

O

P

Q

R